In memory of R' Meir Maimon (z"l)

*This book could not have been written without
the strong foundation given to me by my father,
a source of light to many.*

In memory of Avraham Silver (z"l)

*A special man with very special qualities,
a man who inspired me with his modesty.
He loved Torah, Eretz Yisrael, his friends, and his family.*

*With gratitude to my wife and family
for being the engine and compass behind this book.*

Table Of Contents

Discover The Land Of Israel

Table Of Contents

About The Author

Yossi Maimon was born in divided Jerusalem in 1954. His family lived in the area called "no-mans land," a war zone on the border between Israel and Jordan. When he was three years old, his family moved deeper into the "safe" land, away from the constant attacks of the Jordanian Army.

Yossi was privileged to be one of the first boys to have his Bar Mitzvah in the new courtyard of the Kotel following the 1967 Six Day War, which unified Jerusalem.

Yossi received his education in the Jerusalem school system and joined the army two months before the 1973 Yom Kippur War. He served as a tank commander during his military service.

In 1984, Yossi initiated forming the Yishuv, Maale Levona in the Shomron, where he lives with his family to this day. Yossi describes Maale Levona as "the most beautiful place in Israel."

Since 1986, Yossi has been an active tour guide in Israel, licensed by the Israel Tourism Ministry. As a specialist in Judaic and Middle East Studies, he believes that visitors to *Eretz Yisrael*, the Land of Israel, will come away with a love and better appreciation of the Holy Land when they understand, not only what is happening in the Land today, but the events that happened on the very same ground throughout history as documented in the Bible. It is from this belief that this book series has been written.

Historical Periods

Patriarchs
1948 - 2255 From creation
2057 BCE - 1750 BCE

Exodus
2448 From creation
1550 BCE

Judges
Yehoshua - Shmuel
2488 - 2882 From creation
1510 BCE -1206 BCE

Shaul, David, Shlomo
2830 - 2964 From creation
1194 BCE - 960 BCE

Kings
After the division of Yehuda and Israel
2964 - 3338 From creation
960 BCE - 586 BCE

First Temple Period
2928 - 3338 From creation
996 BCE - 586 BCE

Introduction

As you read the pages of this book, think of yourself in the Land of Israel, in *Eretz HaKodesh*, the Holy Land. Together, we will travel from the Golan Heights in the north of Israel to the Negev in the south. We will stand on the tops of mountains and in the bottoms of valleys looking at the Holy Land that was promised by God to be a Land for the Jewish people.

We will journey on the *Road Of The Patriarchs* from the battlefields of yesterday to modern cities of today so that you can discover the history that happened in each place, maybe hundreds of years apart, that has shaped God's people and their land into who they are today. You will get a feel of what it was like to live with the Patriarchs, the Judges, the Prophets, and the Kings.

Although no one is certain where the exact spots are for some of the stories that take place, we are sure about the general areas. For example, this book does not claim to point you to the very spot where David stood when he shot the stone that killed Goliath, but the vicinity of the battle in Emek Ha'Elah is precise and definite.

Accompanying us, to help us understand this history, will be the holy writings from Tanach, Talmud, and Midrash.

We have incorporated source words from these writings into our stories. As we move between our words and the biblical words of Tanach, Talmud, and Midrash, the font of the text will change.

When the words from Tanach, Talmud, or Midrash are used, you will see the font change to the style you are now reading.

The Sources

In Jewish tradition, the most major event that happened to the Children of Israel after their exodus from Egypt was receiving the Laws of God, the *Torah*.

For 40 days, Moshe learned the Torah on Mount Sinai with God and then brought the Torah down to the Children of Israel.

God's Torah is comprised of both the Written Torah and the Oral Torah. The Oral Torah explains in detail the Written Torah, which is also called the *Chumash*, the Five Books of Moses.

The Torah, together with other Jewish writings of the Bible, is known in Hebrew as *Tanach*. These other Jewish writings are separated between the historical description of Jewish life up to the destruction of the First Temple, while the other part deals with moral and philosophical Jewish wisdom.

Up to the end of the Second Temple period (70 *CE*), the Oral Torah never existed in a written format. It was taught by memory from teacher to student, from father to son. After the fall of the Second Temple and the absolute devastation of Jewish life in the Land of Israel, there was a fear that the surviving Jews would not be able to maintain the study of the Oral Torah and pass this learning on to the future generations.

At this point, Rabbi Yehuda HaNasi, the leader of the generation, gathered all the Rabbis together and compiled all of their Jewish knowledge into two sets of writings. One set is the six books of *Mishna,* which deals with daily Jewish laws. The other set is called *Midrashim*, which includes all the Jewish knowledge and wisdom known at that time.

The meaning of the name Mishna comes from reciting again and again and again the knowledge the student has, in order to carve it into his memory forever. The meaning of Midrashim comes from the wise sayings told by the different Rabbis.

The Mishna includes the principles of Jewish law, but it is written at a very high level. There was a need to simplify these principles into practical daily instructions for the individual and community. This was done through discussions and debates of the Rabbis and became known as the *Talmud*.

In the Mishna, Midrashim, and Talmud, we find many parallel stories to the events that happened in Israel during the time of the Tanach. These stories give a special perspective to the stories described in the Tanach.

Discover
The Land Of Israel

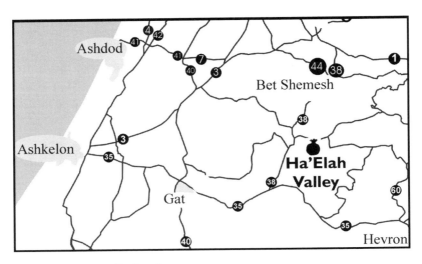

In The Time Of Shaul

Shmuel 1: 17

Ha'Elah Valley

oon after Shaul becomes the first king of Israel, he has to face invading enemy nations that are trying to infiltrate and settle the territory of the Israelite tribes. One of these clashes takes place in the Ha'Elah Valley, which is situated at the crossroads that connects the Judean Hills with the Coastal Plain and the Mediterranean Coast.

Shaul's army positions itself on the hills north of the valley. The mighty armies of the Philistines are camping to the south.

As the battle is set to begin, suddenly a shockwave overcomes the camp of Israel. A man of huge proportions emerges and his appearance causes deep fear amongst the army of Israel.

And there went out a champion from the camp of the Philistines, named Goliath, of Gat, whose height was six cubits and a span. And he had a helmet of copper upon his head, and he was clad with a coat of armor. The weight of the coat was five thousand shekels of brass. He had shields of copper upon his legs and a javelin of copper between his shoulders. The shaft of his spear was like a weaver's beam. His spear's head weighed six hundred shekels of iron. His shield-bearer went before him.

Goliath paces with confidence across the battlefield without fear and his voice thunders across the camp of Israel.

He stood and cried to the armies of Israel, and said to them: "Why do you come out to set your battle in array? Am I not a Philistine, and you servants to Shaul? Choose a man for you, and let him come down to me. If he is able to fight with me, and kill me, then we will be your servants; but if I prevail against him, and kill him, then you will be our servants, and serve us."

For 40 days, Goliath mocks the Israelites. In the morning and in the evening, while the Israelites recite their prayer of *Shema Yisrael*, the prayer that declares the oneness of God, Goliath curses the God of Israel.

The Philistine said: "I do taunt the armies of Israel this day. Give me a man, that we may fight together."

And when Shaul and all Israel heard those words of the Philistine, they were dismayed, and greatly afraid.

King Shaul offers his daughter in marriage and the cancellation of taxes to the family of any man of the Israelite soldiers that will fight Goliath. But no man is prepared to face the Philistine giant.

It happens that a young boy arrives at the camp of Israel with provisions for his brothers as Goliath begins another one of his tirades.

David, the youngest son of Yishai of Beit Lechem (Bethlehem), hears the words of Goliath, words that mock and taunt Israel and their God.

"Who will battle this evil one?" asks little David.

"No one," answer the Israelite soldiers. "Everyone is afraid."

"I'll go," says David. "I'll fight him."

Those around him try to discourage him. "You are only a boy," they tell him, "and Goliath is a man of war."

Quite hard to understand how, but David convinces the soldiers that he can challenge Goliath. So the soldiers bring

David before Shaul, whose first reaction is to doubt that the young boy can face the giant and save Israel.

And Shaul said to David: "You are not able to go against this Philistine to fight with him for you are but a youth and he a man of war from his youth."

Amazingly, David manages to convince the king that he can do the job.

And David said to Shaul: "Your servant kept his father's sheep. When there came a lion, or a bear, and took a lamb out of the flock, I went out after him, and smote him, and delivered it out of his mouth. When he arose against me, I caught him by his beard, and smote him, and slew him.

"Your servant smote both the lion and the bear. This uncircumcised Philistine will be as one of them, seeing he has taunted the armies of the living God."

David said: "The Lord that delivered me out of the paw of the lion, and out of the paw of the bear, He will deliver me out of the hand of this Philistine."

And Shaul said to David: "Go, and the Lord will be with you."

Shaul even offers David his own battle gear. David says no. He has his own weapon – five stones from the River of Nachal.

And that is how David is able to go out to meet Goliath. When Goliath sees Israel's "warrior", he is outraged.

When the Philistine looked and saw David, he detested him for he was only a youth, and ruddy, and with a fair countenance.

The Philistine said to David: "Am I a dog, that you come to me with staves?"

The Philistine cursed David by his god.

The Philistine said to David: "Come to me, and I will give your flesh to the fowls of the air and to the beasts of the field."

David's response to Goliath has become a battle cry for the armies of Israel throughout time.

"You come to me with a sword, and with a spear, and with a javelin. I come to you in the name of the Lord of Hosts, the God of the armies of Israel, whom you have taunted."

And then as swift as lightning...

David put his hand in his bag and took from there a stone and slung it and smote the Philistine in his forehead. The stone sank into his forehead and he fell upon his face to the earth. So David prevailed over the Philistine with a sling and with a stone and smote the Philistine and slew him, but there was no sword in the hand of David.

While we can only imagine the roar of excitement and joy of the Israelite soldiers as they cheered for the young hero, it is quite hard to comprehend the response of King Shaul!

When Shaul saw David go against the Philistine, he said to Avner, his captain: "Avner, whose son is this youth?"

Avner said: "As your soul lives, O king, I cannot tell."

The king said: "Inquire whose son he is."

The Talmud (*Yevamot, p76*) gives us a very special look into the mind of King Shaul, who instead of joining the happiness in the victory of Israel, is busy with a question about David's father.

The Talmud asks how King Shaul does not know David's father, Yishai, who is the head of the *Sanhedrin*, the supreme court of Israel. The Talmud explains that Shaul is actually wondering about another father of David, the father of the house of Yehuda.

The house of Yehuda was built from Zerach and Peretz, the twins of Tamar, who is the daughter-in-law of Yehuda. Zerach would be known as a father of people who would be important, but Peretz would be known as a father of people who would be kings.

Shaul is very concerned because the behavior of David, since the very first moment he met him, strikes him as royal.

...The way he walks...The way he speaks...His confidence. The way David manages to kill Goliath raises the question of whether David is related to Peretz.

Shaul wants to know whether David comes from the house of Peretz or from the house of Zerach. If he comes from Zerach, he has been granted to be a great man, but no more. And that's fine in the eyes of Shaul. But, if he comes from Peretz, clearly David is a threat to Shaul's throne. That is what is bothering Shaul and is the reason that he did not celebrate with Israel.

In order to address this question, Avner has to go to the house of study to figure out the answer. But another advisor to Shaul, Doeg HaEdomi, turns to the king and says, "You are busy with the question about his father, but first you should ask a more important question – Is David a Jew?" Doeg knows that David's great grandmother is Ruth the Moabite, so he thinks that he had found a loophole to prevent David from becoming King.

It is said in the Torah *(Ki Tetze, 23:4)* that...

An Ammonite or Moabite will not enter the congregation of God."

So the scholars in the house of study had to examine whether this question referred to men and women or to men only.

To understand this question, we have to go back to the time of the Exodus from Egypt. The Talmud explains that when the Israelites were traveling in the desert after the leaving Egypt, they needed to cross the land of Moab on their way to the Land of Israel. But the Moabites refused to let them cross and did not provide them with bread and water.

So the Talmud concludes that since men are responsible for hosting guests, only men are included in the prohibition.

From this discussion we know that David is a true son

of Israel, as he was the descendant of a Moabite woman that became Jewish, and also a descendant of Peretz.

As time goes by, David becomes a successful officer in the army of Shaul and gains popularity. At the same time, King Shaul continues to see David as a possible usurper of his throne.

The daughters of Israel sing the song "Shaul has fought thousands, and David tens of thousands." This brings out Shaul's hatred and jealousy toward David, so much so that it causes him to seek out David to kill him.

So now we understand how Shaul's hatred for David is sparked, a hatred that plagues David until Shaul's death.

The mighty battle between David and Goliath is not simply a confrontation on the battlefield, but an encounter with a deeper meaning. It can be revealed by looking at the ancestry of these two men.

David is the great grandson of Ruth the Moabite, the daughter of Eglon, who is the King of Moab. Ruth's sister is Orpah. The two sisters are married to Machlon and Kielyon, the sons of Elimelech, who is the husband of Naomi.

In the story from Megilat Ruth, it is told that after the death of Elimelech and the death of his sons, Naomi is left alone with her daughters-in-law. Naomi decides to return to the land of Yehuda. She pleads with the sisters to return to the house of their father, a royal house in Moab. But Ruth clings to Naomi, and becomes a Jew, whereas Orpah returns to Moab, to her idol-worshipping father.

While it is clear that David is a descendent of Ruth, we learn from the Talmud that Goliath is a descendant of Orpah – David's great aunt. So on a different level, it turns out that the battle between Goliath and David is also a battle between two cousins, between two philosophies, between two beliefs. *(Sota 42)*

Each one represents a separate spiritual world, a legacy passed on by the choices of their foremothers. Goliath represents idol worship. David represents the belief in One God. And the description in the Tanach reflects this.

This day the Lord will deliver you into my hand. I will kill you, and take your head off from you. I will give the carcasses of the host of the Philistines this day to the fowls of the air and to the wild beasts of the earth so that all the earth may know that there is a God in Israel.

It is interesting to note that at the same time that the battle is about to start, another event takes place that is going to affect David's life later.

Goliath has a special soldier who carries his shield, which is large and heavy. Only a strong warrior can carry it.

His shield-bearer went before him.

The Zohar *(c206, s1)* reveals that before the battle begins, David makes an offer to the man who carries the shield of Goliath, saying, "If you will be on my side in the battle against Goliath and become a Jew, I will give you one of the daughters of Israel." As a result of the battle, the shield-bearer becomes a Jew, recognizing that God is the true God of Israel. And later he marries Bat Sheva. The shield-bearer is none other than Uriah the Hittite.

The Zohar explains that God punishes David for treating the daughters of Israel so cheaply, by offering them to strangers – offering something that is not his. Therefore God takes the woman who was originally meant to be for David and gives her instead, to Uriah as his wife.

Only afterwards, with a lot of pain and sorrow, Bat Sheva becomes David's wife. She is the mother of Shlomo, who builds the First Temple of God in Jerusalem. The story of how Bat Sheva becomes David's wife is told in Shmuel 2, chapter 11.

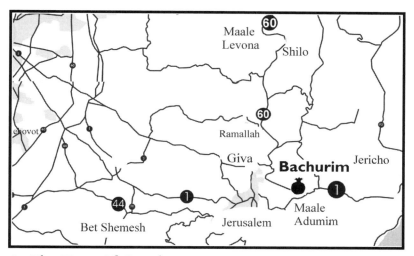

In The Time Of David
Shmuel 2: 15, 16, 19 ~ Kings 1: 2

Bachurim

W hen you drive east from Jerusalem towards Jericho, to the desert of Benjamin, you will pass by
the city of Maale Adumim. This is the area where
the city of Bachurim was once located, where
the desert hills surround you, and the Bedouin flocks of goats
and sheep are trying to eat something on the desolate landscape.
This is the place where one of the most impressive stories from
the life of David takes place.

In the last year of his life, David had hoped to spend
some time learning and relaxing. The man, who never knew
one day of rest, hopes to add quiet to a lifetime of struggle and
war.

All of a sudden...

*There came a messenger to David, saying: "The hearts of
the men of Israel are after Avshalom."*

The message is very clear. Avshalom, son of David,
has managed to build an army and he is on his way to conquer
Jerusalem. Now David must make a decision whether to fight
the traitors led by his son or avoid the battle and flee Jerusalem.

David has no doubts...

*And David said to all his servants that were with him in
Jerusalem: "Arise, and let us flee or else none of us shall escape*

from Avshalom. Make speed to depart, or he will overtake us quickly, and bring down evil upon us, and smite the city with the edge of the sword."

David takes off his crown and shoes, and with a heavy heart, walks out of his city. The Kohen Gadol, Zadok, together with the Levites, suggests to David that the Ark of the Covenant should escort the King, thinking that whoever has the Ark, has God with him.

And the King said to Zadok: "Carry back the Ark of God into the city. If I shall find favor in the eyes of the Lord, He will bring me back, and show me both it, and His city. But if He says 'I have no delight in you,' behold, here am I, let Him do to me as it seems good to Him."

And David, surrounded with his loyal servants and army, walks out to exile towards Jericho.

And all the country wept with a loud voice, as all the people passed over and as the king passed over the brook Kidron, all the people passed over, toward the way of the wilderness.

On the way to exile, the mourning convoy passes the Benjamin city, Bachurim. One of the most important people in this city, Shim'ee, son of Gera approaches the king.

When King David came to Bachurim, behold, there came out a man of the family of the house of Shaul, whose name was Shim'ee, the son of Gera. He came out and kept on cursing as he came.

He cast stones at David, and at all the servants of King David and all the people and all the mighty men were on his right hand and on his left. Then Shim'ee said when he cursed: "Go, Go, you, man of blood, and base fellow. The Lord has returned upon you all the blood of the house of Shaul, in whose stead you have reigned. The Lord has delivered the kingdom into the hand of Avshalom your son. Behold, you are taken in your own mischief, because you are a man of blood."

Shim'ee, who sees the king fleeing his city, thinks that

now is the right time to bring back the crown to the house of Shaul, and so that is the reason for his behavior.

David, who is surrounded with his men, could easily kill Shim'ee, as one of his heroes, Avishai ben Zurya suggests.

Then Avishai the son of Zurya said to the king: "Why should this dead dog curse my lord the king? Let me go over and take off his head."

And David answered...

"My son, who came forth from my body, seeks my life. How much more this Benjamite now? Leave him alone, and let him curse for the Lord has told him.

"It may be that the Lord will see the tear in my eye and that the Lord will repay me with good for his cursing me this day."

David ignores Shim'ee and he continues to walk to exile, cursed and humiliated.

Three months later, there is a battle between David's supporters and the army of Avshalom. The revolt comes to an end after Avshalom is killed. The people of Israel invite David to return to Jerusalem.

And all the people discussed with all the tribes of Israel, saying: "The king delivered us out of the hand of our enemies. He saved us out of the hand of the Philistines. Now he has fled the land from Avshalom. And Avshalom, whom we anointed over us, is dead in battle. Now, therefore, why are you silent about bringing the king back?"

And just before David is about to cross the Jordan River on his way back to Jerusalem...

Shim'ee the son of Gera, the Benjamite, who was of Bachurim, made haste and came down with the men of Yehuda to meet King David. Shim'ee the son of Gera fell down before the king, when he would go over the Jordan.

And he said to the king: "Let my lord not impute iniquity to me, neither do you remember what your servant did iniquitously the day that my lord the king went out of Jerusalem, that the king should take it to his heart for your servant knows that I have sinned. Therefore, behold, I have come this day, the first of all the house of Joseph to go down to meet my lord the king."

David is standing in front of the man who cursed him, spit on him, and stoned him on his way to exile, who is now asking for forgiveness.

But Avishai the son of Zurya answered and said: "Shall not Shim'ee be put to death for this, because he cursed the Lord's anointed?"

David ignores the opinion of his men and he promises Shim'ee...

"You shall not die." And the king swore to him.

According to the Talmud, David not only forgives Shim'ee for cursing him, but makes quite an amazing request. *(Brachot 8)* "Would you be the teacher of my son, Shlomo, who is going to be the next king of Israel?"

And so Shim'ee agrees and becomes the teacher of Shlomo and prepares him for the kingship over Israel and building the First Temple.

A few months later, David is about to die and passes his crown to his son, Shlomo.

Now the days of David drew near that he should die.

Among his instructions, David tells Shlomo...

"There is with you Shim'ee the son of Gera, the Benjamite, of Bachurim, who cursed me with a grievous curse in the day when I went to Machanaim. But he came down to meet me at the Jordan, and I swore to him by the Lord, saying: 'I will not put you to death with the sword.'"

Now therefore you should not hold him guiltless, for you are a wise man and you will know what to do to him. You shall bring his white hair to the grave with blood."

David's behavior seems quite strange. On one hand, David forgives Shim'ee for cursing him and even offers him a job which most likely would be offered to someone close to the king, serving as the teacher of his son, the next king of Israel.

So how is it that on the other hand, David instructs his son to kill his teacher, Shim'ee?

It doesn't seem to make sense!

The Talmud (*Megila p12*) helps us to understand the King's strange order to his son.

The Talmud says to look at the difference between the two kings, Shaul and David.

What makes David better to replace Shaul? The Talmud reminds us that Shaul, as king of Israel, had been ordered by God to wipe out Amalek, and all that belonged to Amalek. But Shaul did not follow God's order and spared the animals and the life of the king of Amalek, Agog. The Talmud then asks, What lineage came from Agog? It was Haman, who planned to kill all of the Jews, as we know from the Purim story in Megilat Ester.

David, under the circumstances of Bachurim, as the king of Israel, had every right to kill Shim'ee and he did not. The Talmud explains that from the lineage of Shim'ee came Mordechai, who saved the Jews from Haman.

...A Jewish man was in the capital, Shushan and his name is Mordechai, son of Yair, son of Shim'ee, son of Kish, a Benjamite man. (Megilat Ester: 2;5)

It was Mordechai who orchestrated Haman's defeat and ultimately saw him hang from the gallows.

David understands that although he was cursed and stoned by Shim'ee, Shim'ee is actually a great man who made a mistake. Cursing the king deserves death, but it is not yet Shim'ee's time to die. And so by not killing Shim'ee, David assures the future of Israel.

David could not kill Shim'ee because he knew that he will have important descendants. This is the reason why David does not kill him. So when David is about to die, he instructs Shlomo to kill Shim'ee and tells him when to do it.

David tells Shlomo to kill Shim'ee only after he is too old to have more children, to be sure that all of his children have been born.

By ordering Shlomo to kill this man, David makes sure that Shim'ee will pay his debt in this world and be able to enter *Olam Haba,* the world to come. In this way David takes care of Shim'ee's future.

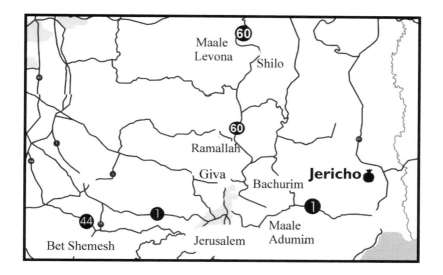

In The Time Of The Kings

Yehoshua: 2, 6 ~ Kings I: 16, 17 ~ Devarim: 11

Jericho

When you read the book of Kings I in the Tanach, you will find a chapter that deals with a description of the kings of Yehuda and the kings of Israel. It concludes by describing the evil ways of King Achav, who is married to a gentile woman named Ezevel.

And it came to pass, as if it had been a light thing for him to walk in the sins of Yerovam, the son of Nevat, that he married Ezevel, the daughter of Etbaal, king of the Tzidonians, and went and served Baal, and worshipped him.

In the middle of the description, the Tanach draws our attention to something that seems irrelevant and not connected to the issue being dealt with.

In his days, Hiel the Bethelite built Jericho. With Aviram his firstborn, he laid the foundation there, and with his youngest son Segev, he set up the gates there, according to the word of the Lord, which He spoke by the hand of Yehoshua, the son of Nun.

While we are trying to understand the connection between building Jericho in the time of Achav, the Tanach throws us into another story, which again seems disconnected.

And Eliyahu the Tishbi, who was of the settlers of Gilad, said to Achav: "As the Lord, the God of Israel, lives, before whom I stand, there shall not be dew or rain these years, unless I say so."

So what is the connection?

The Talmud gives us the story behind this story to understand the Tanach.

But in order to understand the Tanach, we have to go back to the time of Yehoshua, who leads the people of Israel into the Promised Land.

The first challenge facing Yehoshua is to conquer the city of Jericho.

Jericho is known as the gate to Israel. On the exterior, it is a very strong city that is flourishing in the desert as it is located on an oasis that enjoys the irrigation of three sources of water. Jericho's king has managed to build a massive, invincible wall around the city for its protection.

As the commander of the Israelite Army, Yehoshua develops a plan to conquer which first involves sending in spies. The Tanach presents an entire chapter describing their mission.

The spies find themselves in the house of a woman named Rachav, who describes the real atmosphere of the city.

She said to the men: "I know that the Lord has given you the land, and fear of you has fallen on us, and all the inhabitants of the land melt away before you.

"We have heard how the Lord dried up the water of the Red Sea before you, when you came out of Egypt and what you did to the two kings of the Amorites, that were beyond the Jordan, and to Sihon and to Og, whom you totally destroyed.

"As soon as we had heard it, our hearts did melt. There did not remain any more spirit in any man, because of you for the Lord your God, He is God in heaven above, and on earth beneath."

The two spies promise Rachav to save whoever is in her house when the city is conquered. Through the window, they leave the city and return back to Yehoshua, reporting the encouraging information.

The story of Yehoshua conquering Jericho is a unique one because the city is conquered without using any conventional fighting methods.

And the Lord said to Yehoshua: "See, I have given into your hand Jericho, and the king who is there, even the mighty men of valor.

"And you shall circle the city, all the men of war, going around the city once. This shall you do for six days."

The instructions are very clear. For six days the army of Israel is to circle the city, one time, led by the Ark of the Covenant with seven Kohanim carrying seven shofars, walking before the Ark. The whole operation is to be done in absolute silence.

And Yehoshua commanded the people, saying: "You shall not shout, nor let your voice be heard, neither shall any word proceed out of your mouth, until the day I tell you to shout. Then you shall shout."

This behavior of Israel looks strange, even eerie. Probably from the point of view of the fighters on the wall of Jericho, it even looks scary.

Yes, that's the whole point. Jericho, as the first city facing Israel, gets special treatment by God. In this battle, there are no swords or spears, nothing of a conventional nature that will be used the future battles of Israel.

On the seventh day...

They rose early at the dawning of the day, and circled the city in the same manner, seven times. Only on that day they circled the city seven times.

When Yehoshua gives the sign...

The people shouted, and the Kohanim blew with the shofars. And it came to pass, when the people heard the sound of the shofars, that the people shouted with a great shout, and the wall fell down flat, so that the people went up into the city, every man straight before him, and they took the city.

From the whole city, the only people who were saved were Rachav and her family. The city was burned. All of its possessions were dedicated to God. On the ruins of the city, Yehoshua stands and swears...

"Cursed be the man before the Lord that rises up and builds this city, even Jericho.

For 400 years the city of Jericho is left in ruins and deserted as a memorial to the miraculous way God gave this Land to the Children of Israel. But now after 400 years, a man from the city Beit El, named Hiel, thinks that enough time has passed since the curse and that it is time to develop the economic potential of Jericho.

So Hiel goes to Jericho and rebuilds the city.

And just as Yehoshua ben Nun cursed...

With the loss of his firstborn when he shall lay the foundation, and with the loss of his youngest son when he shall set up the gates...

...Hiel's sons die and he observes *shiva*, the seven days of mourning for them.

At this point, God turns to Eliyahu, who at this time is an unknown Prophet and asks him to go down to Jericho and convey his condolence to Hiel.

Eliyahu, who knows Hiel is an idol worshiper, does not like the idea of going to visit Hiel in Jericho. He says to God, "I'm not so comfortable going to this man, who is known as an idol worshiper."

But God explains that right now there is another man on his way to Jericho to convey his condolence to Hiel, the king of Israel, Achav. And God says, "I want you to be there to give the Jewish reason for Hiel's tragedy."

When Eliyahu hears that Hiel and Achav are going to

be there together, he rejects God's request, saying, "I know for sure that they are going to speak bad of You. Definitely I do not want to go to Jericho. And God says, "Go. And if they will speak against Me, whatever you will say, I will comply."

And so Eliyahu obeys the request of God to go to Jericho. While he is sitting together with Hiel and Achav, Hiel starts complaining that his sons died, due to the curse of Yehoshua.

King Achav hushes Hiel saying, " Your sons did not die because of any curse. It was a tragic coincidence that has nothing to do with the curse of Yehoshua."

Hiel says, "My sons died exactly the way Yehoshua predicted. The oldest, Aviram, when I was laying the foundations and my youngest son, Segev, when I set up the gates.

King Achav says, "I can prove to you that the sons died of natural reasons and not because of any curse.

"Would you please tell me who was greater, Moshe or Yehoshua?

"The answer is that because Yehoshua was the student, Moshe, the teacher had to be greater. Moshe said in the Torah in part of *Shema Yisrael...*

Be careful not to let your heart be deceived, and leave the path of God, and serve other gods, and worship them. The anger of the Lord will be kindled against you and He will close the heaven so that there shall be no rain and the ground shall not yield her fruit and you will perish quickly from off the good land which the Lord gives you.

Achav continues to explain that long before the time of Yehoshua, his teacher, Moshe, cursed the sky not to rain, and the earth not to grow any crops if the sons of Israel worship idols.

"Take a look at me," says Achav. "I worship all kinds of idols and the rain has not stopped and the land continues to give good food. So if the curse of Moshe, the teacher, did not happen, why should the curse of his student Yehoshua happen? "You can be sure that your sons died of an accident and not of Yehoshua's curse."

At this point, Eliyahu interrupts saying...

"As the Lord, the God of Israel lives, before whom I stand, there shall not be dew or rain these years, unless I say so."

Eliyahu, according to the agreement he had with God, is free to do whatever he decides and God will make it happen.

When Eliyahu sees that Achav is not only proud of worshiping idols, but is also confident that the rain will not stop and the good life will continue, the Prophet gets so angry with the king that he promises there will be no rain unless Achav repents.

The words of Eliyahu do not instill fear in anyone. Still no one knows his power as a Prophet. Achav does not give any attention to what Eliyahu has just said and he returns back to his city, Shomron, the capital of Israel.

Eliyahu goes to the Crete Valley, east of the Jordan River, to find shelter from the king. He will soon realize that the character of the weather has changed and that there is no rain.

In the valley, ravens will bring him food. And from the river, he will drink.

So he went and did according to the word of the Lord and dwelt by the brook Crete, that is before the Jordan.

We learn that the food that was brought by the ravens was taken from the table of King Yehoshafat in Jerusalem. *(Midrash Bamidbar Raba 23:9)*

And the ravens brought him bread and meat in the morning, and bread and meat in the evening. He drank from the brook.

Even today Israel is a country that relies on rain. The immediate effect of no rain means no food, hunger, and people dying.

God, who sees the people suffering the effects of no rain, turns to Eliyahu asking him to bring back the rain.

Eliyahu responds, "You and I made an agreement. What I will say, You will do. Achav, who spoke against you in the house of Hiel in Jericho, must repent before I bring back the rain."

God sees that Eliyahu is stubborn and does not understand the misery of the people. So God dries up the source of Eliyahu's water in the Crete River.

After a while, the brook dried up, because there was no rain in the land.

Maybe this will influence the Prophet to bring back the rain. But Eliyahu is firm. The rain will not return until Achav repents.

God understands that Eliyahu needs special treatment to convince him to relent. So He sends him on a mission to Tzor that will ultimately force him to bring back the rain.

"Arise, go to Tzor, which is close to Tzidon, and dwell there. Behold, I have commanded a widow there to host you."

Now, we are able to see the connection between what appears to be a series of unconnected events.

In the time of King Achav, one of the major events that takes place is the rebuilding of the city of Jericho by Hiel.

Hiel's sons die under unusual circumstances and Achav comes to comfort his friend.

God sends Eliyahu to give his condolence to Hiel. Eliyahu reacts to Achav's attitude and his worship of idols by withholding the rain.

The story of how the rain is eventually brought back by Eliyahu after Achav repents is found in the story of the city of Tzor and Mount Carmel.

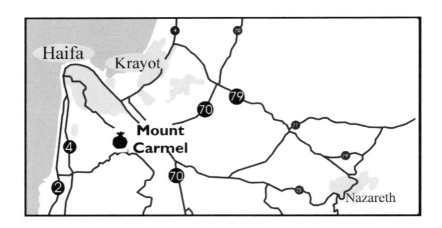

In The Time Of The Kings
Kings 1: 18, 19

Mount Carmel

It has been three years since the last rain fell in Israel. The drought brings the country to disaster. Even King Achav is worried.

Achav said to Ovadyahu: "Go through the land, to all the springs of water, and to all the brooks. Maybe we will find grass to keep the horses and mules alive, so that we will not lose the animals." So they divided the land between them, to pass through it: Achav went one way by himself and Ovadyahu went another way by himself.

Ovadyahu is...

In charge of the household.

Actually Ovadyahu is the minister in charge of all the financial activities for Achav. If the king himself and his minister take personal measures, it looks like things are really bad.

Ovadyahu, on his way, sees...

Eliyahu is in front of him. He knew him and fell on his face and said: "Is it you, my master, Eliyahu?"

Eliyahu is very busy thinking about his life project, bringing Achav to repentance. He has no time for small talk.

The answer is sharp.

"It is me. Go and tell your lord. Eliyahu is here."

Ovadyahu does not understand. Why would Eliyahu want to meet Achav, who wants to kill him? Eliyahu should run away. And what about me?

"What have I done to you that you deliver your servant into the hand of Achav, to kill me?

"As the Lord lives, there is no nation or kingdom, where my lord has not sent to look for you. When they said: 'He is not here, he took an oath of the kingdom and nation, if they find you.'"

"When Achav finds out that I have met with you and did not kill you, he will kill me."

According to the Midrash, the days of King Achav were very special days. Though people were worshiping idols, they would not speak evil against each other and would not betray one another to the authorities.

This kind of behavior was so common that the knowledge about the 100 men Ovadyahu, the minister of Achav, was hiding, did not seep to his King Achav.

This behavior also had quite an unbelievable effect in the wars Achav conducted – There were no casualties for the troops of Israel.

Unlike the time of King David, when people were righteous and very learned, but still spoke evil against each other, there was the opposite effect. In the wars David commanded, there were many casualties. *(Devarim Raba, c5, s6)*

"As soon as I leave you, the spirit of the Lord will carry you to an unknown place. So when I come and tell Achav, and he will not find you, he will kill me."

Ovadyahu tries to explain to Eliyahu, "I might be a minister in the house of Achav, but I am a secret true believer in the God of Israel. In fact...

"When Ezevel killed the prophets of the Lord, I hid a hundred prophets of the Lord - fifty in a cave, and fed them with bread and water."

Do not take me as one of Achav's people, because...

I, your servant, feared the Lord from my youth.

Even Eliyahu mistakenly thinks that he is the last God-fearing man left in Israel.

"I have been very jealous for the Lord, the God of hosts, for the Children of Israel have forsaken Your covenant, thrown down Your altars, and killed Your prophets with the sword. Only I am left and they seek my life, to take it away."

And Eliyahu answers...

"As the Lord of hosts lives, before whom I stand, I will surely show myself to him today."

So Achav arrives and as he see Eliyahu, he says...

"Is it you, the destroyer of Israel?"

Eliyahu answers...

"I have not troubled Israel. But you and your father's house have, because you have forsaken the commandments of the Lord and have followed the Baalim.

And here Eliyahu plays his card...

He turns to Achav saying, "Achav, I know that you are a good man. The people around you misled you to go the wrong way. I am going to offer you a deal. Let's have a test and see which God can bring fire from heaven. If you win, I'll become an idol worshiper. But if I win, you will have to believe in the God of Israel..."

"So gather all Israel at Mount Carmel and the prophets of Baal, four hundred and fifty, and the prophets of the Asherah four hundred, that eat at Ezevel's table."

Achav accepts the challenge.

Achav sent for all the Children of Israel and gathered the prophets together at Mount Carmel.

Eliyahu is really a master showman. The show he is conducting now will affect every person in Israel. This is the reason why Eliyahu is organizing a monumental presentation, which attracts everybody, from everywhere in Israel.

Eliyahu came to all the people and said: "How long will you walk between the two paths? If the Lord is the real God, follow Him. But if Baal is, follow him."

The question remains in the air...

And the people did not answer him.

The terms of the test are simple...

"Give us two bulls. Let them choose one bull for themselves. Cut it into pieces and lay it on the wood. Put no fire under it. I will cut the other bull and lay it on the wood and put no fire under it."

Then...

"You shall call the name of your god, and I will call the name of the Lord."

And...

"The God that answers by fire, is the real God."

This time...

The people answered and said: "It is well spoken."

The atmosphere is now electrified. On the slopes of the mountain, all of Israel is sitting. In front of them, the alters. One, surrounded with 450 pagan prophets, while near the other one is only one man, Eliyahu...

Eliyahu said to the prophets of Baal: "Choose one bull for yourselves and cut it first, for you are many. Call on the name of your god, but put no fire under it."

So the pagan prophets...

...took the bull which was given to them and cut it and called on the name of Baal from morning even until noon, saying: "O Baal, answer us." But there was no answer. They danced by the altar that was made.

After awhile, Eliyahu starts teasing them...

"Cry out loud for he is a god. Either he is meditating, or he has gone aside, or he is on a journey, or maybe he is asleep and must be awaked."

And so...

They cried out loud, and cut themselves, according to their

custom, with swords and lances, until blood gushed out on them.
When midday passed, they prophesied until the time of the offering of the evening offering.

Yet...

There was neither voice nor any answer nor any listener.

Now Eliyahu turns to the people saying...

"Come to me." All the people came to him. He repaired the altar of the Lord that was destroyed.

Eliyahu shows the importance of the unity of Israel by...

Taking twelve stones, according to the number of the tribes of the sons of Yaakov, to whom the word of the Lord came, saying: "Israel shall be your name."

And with the stones, he built an altar in the name of the Lord.

And now, in order not to give any excuse to anybody...

He made a trench around the altar, as great as would contain two measures of seed.

"Fill four jars with water and pour it on the burnt offering and on the wood." And then he said: "Do it the second time." And they did it the second time. And he said: "Do it the third time." And they did it the third time.

And the water ran around the altar. He filled the trench also with water.

Now even the cynics cannot say it was a hot day and that it was a spark that started the fire. There is water everywhere.

The time has come for the moment of truth.

At the time of the offering of the evening offering, Eliyahu the prophet came near and said: "O Lord, the God of Avraham, of Yitzhok, and of Israel, let it be known this day that You are God in Israel and that I am Your servant, and that I have done all these things according to Your word.

"Answer me, O Lord, answer me, that this people may know that You, Lord, are God, for You did turn their heart backward."

All of a sudden...

Fire of the Lord fell and consumed the burnt offering, and the wood, and the stones, and the dust, and licked up the water that was in the trench.

The vision is shocking...

The people saw it and they fell on their faces saying: "The Lord, He is God, the Lord. He is God."

Eliyahu, a man of revenge, takes advantage of a rare moment and he orders...

"Take the prophets of Baal. Do not let any of them escape." So they took them and Eliyahu brought them down to the brook Kishon and slaughtered them there.

For Eliyahu, the mission has been accomplished. King Achav, who witnessed the unbelievable miracle, repents according to the deal he had with Eliyahu. Now Eliyahu can bring the rain back.

So he turns to Achav...

"Get up, eat and drink, for there is the sound of abundant rain."

Eliyahu knows that the road from Mount Carmel to Achav's palace in Yizrael will become unmarchable when the rain begins. So he warns Achav...

"Get your chariot ready and go down, so that the rain will not stop you."

To honor and respect the king of Israel, who just repented...

The hand of the Lord was on Eliyahu. He girded up his loins and ran before Achav to the entrance of Yizrael.

For Eliyahu, this is the sweet moment he has been waiting to see for three years. It all started when he was asked by God to go to Jericho to give his condolences to Hiel, the builder of new Jericho, who lost his two sons by the curse of Yehoshua.

And Yehoshua swore at that time saying, "Cursed before the Lord be the man who rises up and rebuilds this city Jericho.

With his oldest he will lay the foundation. With his youngest, he will set up its gates."

During the visit in the house of Hiel, King Achav, Hiel's friend, tries to prove that the deaths of Hiel's sons were a natural accident and did not happen because of any curse.

Angered, Eliyahu promises that there will be no rain, as long as Achav worships idols.

For three years Eliyahu and Achav chase each other. Achav wants to kill Eliyahu for stopping the rain. Eliyahu wants Achav to regret his idol worship. Eliyahu wins the game after he manages to organize the test of fire that impresses all Israel, including King Achav. It is under these circumstances that Achav admits that the God of Israel is the only real God.

And now Eliyahu brings the rain back, as he promised God in Tzor when the son of the widow was revived.

This pleasing moment did not last very long. When Ezevel, the wife of Achav, hears what happened, she...

...sent a messenger to Eliyahu, saying: "So the gods will help me, tomorrow I will put your life as the life of one of them."

Once again Eliyahu is running for his life.

On the top of Mount Carmel, where a high antenna stands today, about two miles east of Haifa University, there is a place where we believe this story happened. From this location, which is probably the place where Eliyahu prayed for the rain, we can see both the brook of Kishon in the northeast and the Mediterranean Sea in the southwest.

Eliyahu went up to the top of Carmel. He bowed down to the earth and put his face between his knees.

He said to his servant: "Go up now, look toward the sea."

And he went up and looked and said: "There is nothing."

And he said: "Go again seven times."

At the seventh time, he said: "Behold, a cloud arose out of the sea, as small as a man's hand."

He said: "Go up, say to Achav: 'Get your chariot ready and get yourself down, so that the rain will not stop you.'"

A short while later, the sky became black with clouds and wind.

There was a great rain.

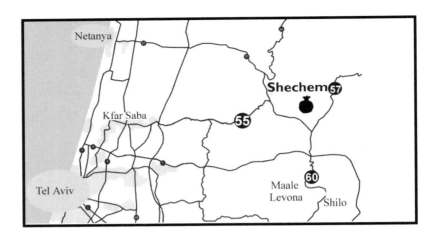

In The Time Of The Patriarchs
Beresheet: 12, 34, 35

Shechem

The mountainous region that is known today as the Shomron starts in Beit El in the south and goes up to the valley of Yizrael, its northern border. This area is connected by a major road known as the Road Of The Patriarchs, which originates from the stories in the book of *Beresheet* (Genesis) when the Patriarchs traveled throughout the land promised to them by God, from north to south, back and forth. This road was the most comfortable geographic pathway to the entire region, woven through the mountains, making the way for the traveler solid and easy.

The city of Shechem, which used to be the capital of the whole region, is centrally positioned in these mountains. The city was known as the center for two very powerful Israelite tribes, Efraim and Menashe, who were the sons of Yosef. They were uniquely apportioned by Yaakov to be counted as two separate tribes and became the leaders of the kingdom of Israel after the split from the kingdom of Yehuda.

The first time the city of Shechem is mentioned in the Torah involves Avraham, the father of the Jewish people.

Avraham (Avram), who could have been the first research scientist in the world because of the way he viewed the world, tries to grasp what the real position is of every object in the vast universe. He searches for the real superpower who controls nature. Ultimately, he comes to the conclusion that it is the hidden and unseen Almighty God who directs the world. At this point, God tells Avraham to come to His House.

"Go for yourself from your country and from your relatives, and from your father's house, to the land that I will show you."

Avraham does not question God and follows Him to the Land.

And Avram took Sarai his wife, and Lot his brother's son, and all their possessions that they had gathered, and the souls that they had gotten in Haran. They went into the land of Canaan."

Seventy five years old, Avraham makes *aliya*. He comes to the Land. On his journey...

Avram passes through the Land to the place of Shechem, to the plain of Moreh. And the Canaanite was then in the Land.

We can imagine how excited Avraham is to know that this Land is the Land of God, the most blessed and holy piece of land in the entire world. And this Land will belong to his descendants. So...

The Lord appeared to Avram, and said: "To your seed will I give this land." And he built there an altar to the Lord who appeared to him.

The first sacrifice Avraham offers to God is in Shechem. According to the Talmud, *(Sota 10)* wherever Avraham camps, he starts a *Yeshiva*, a place where people can come to ask, explore, and learn about the new concept of believing in the hidden, spiritual God. The first Yeshiva Avraham opens is in Shechem.

The next time Shechem appears in the Torah is in the story of Avraham's grandson, Yaakov. After 22 years as a refugee, Yaakov returns back to his fatherland, escorted with 11 sons, one daughter, and livestock and possessions.

Yaakov came in peace to the city of Shechem, which is in the land of Canaan, when he came from Paddan Aram and camped before the city.

According to the Talmud, when Yaakov arrives in Shechem, he pauses and takes a big, relaxing breath. After all, this chased-after person, 22 years ago had to flee from his home and has now returned back – safe, rich, and the head of a large family. All of this is in spite of the people that he has had to deal with during these long years. There was Lavan, who tried in every possible way to cheat and take whatever he managed to gain. And there was his cruel brother Esav, who simply sought his blood and wanted to kill him.

> According to the Midrash, only Yosef's spiritual personality can challenge Esav, Yaakov's most serious fear.
> *(Beresheet Raba 73:5)*

Yaakov understands how big the wall of protection is that God has built to keep him safe from these people all these years, so he gives thanks to God in a special way.

Yaakov offers his services, for free, to help the community of Shechem. First, he creates reliable weights and measures for the people so that they can trade with honesty. And then he teaches how to slaughter animals in a kosher way, so that the people can have kosher meat to eat.

The idea behind providing these services is twofold. First, Yaakov wants to spread the story of God and to thank Him in public so that people will come and ask why he does these good deeds for the people. This way Yaakov will be able to say that God treats him properly and this is his way of thanking Him. Second, this is a way that the name of God can be spread among a much wider group of people who have benefited from these services.

Then Yaakov does something quite strange.

He bought the parcel of ground, where he had spread his tent at the hand of the children of Hamor, Shechem's father, for a hundred pieces of money.

Why does Yaakov need to buy this piece of land?

...To be a final resting place for his son, Yosef, who is not yet five years old.

So what kind of father buys a burial site for his healthy little boy? ...A father who knows something that we do not know.

As soon as Yosef is born, God turns to Yaakov and says, "It is time to return home. Do not fear. Yosef is with you and he will help you deal with the problem of Esav." This promise comes true when Yaakov and his family survive the meeting with Esav while on the way to the Land of Israel.

As Yaakov enters the Land of Israel, the first thing he does is purchase a piece of land for his son's burial, although

---

After the Egyptians realized the severity of the plague of the death of the firstborn, the people of Israel receive the order from Pharaoh, "Leave Egypt immediately."

Slavery for the Israelites is about to end. The people have a very short time to prepare for the Exodus.

Moshe takes this opportunity to go and look Yosef's coffin. Witnesses had reported that the Egyptians buried Yosef in the Nile River, thinking that they would be blessed, since the Nile is a source of life for them.

Moshe went to the Nile and called, "Yosef! Yosef! The time has come for the people of Israel to leave Egypt. Appear now so that we can take you with us. Either you show up now or we are free of your vow."

According to the Midrash, the beautifully decorated, heavy silver coffin pops to the surface of the water and the people of Israel carry it to the Land of Israel. *(Sota 13)*

Yosef is still very young. Yaakov knows that only when Yosef's bones are buried in the soil of this Land, no matter what the future brings, Esav will never have a hold in the Land of Israel.

This is the reason why when it is time for the Israelites to leave Egypt...

Moshe took the bones of Yosef with him for he had firmly sworn to the Children of Israel, saying: "God will surely remember you and you shall carry up my bones away from here with you." (Shemot: 13;19)

Despite the haste to leave Egypt, Moshe remembers to search for the coffin of Yosef, who is buried in the Nile River. The people of Israel carry this coffin for 40 years in the desert until they bring it to the very place that Yaakov bought for his beloved son to be buried.

And the bones of Yosef, which the Children of Israel brought up out of Egypt, they buried in Shechem, in the parcel of ground which Yaakov bought from the sons of Hamor, the father of Shechem, for a hundred pieces of money. And they became the inheritance of the Children of Yosef. (Yehoshua: 24;32)

Yaakov is not able to sit quietly for very long...

Dinah, the daughter of Leah, whom she had born to Yaakov, went out to see the daughters of the land. Shechem, the son of Hamor the Hivite, the prince of the land, saw her and he took her and lay with her and abused her.

Now he has serious plans regarding Dinah.

Shechem spoke to his father Hamor, saying: "Get me this girl for a wife."

Yaakov knows what happened and he waits quietly for his sons.

Hamor, the father of Shechem went out to Yaakov to speak with him.

When the brothers arrive...

They were grieved and they were very angry because he had brought shame in Israel to lay with Yaakov's daughter.

Hamor begins the negotiations, saying...

"The soul of my son Shechem longs for your daughter. Please give her to him for a wife. Make you marriages with us. Give your daughters to us and take our daughters for you. You shall sit with us and the land shall be for you. Trade and dwell there on it."

Shechem said to her father and her brothers: "Let me find favor in your eyes and what you shall say to me, I will give. Increase gifts on me and I will give according as you shall say to me, but give me the girl for a wife."

The brothers decide to refuse by demanding a very high condition. They think he will never accept...

"We cannot do this, to give our sister to one that is uncircumcised for that is a disgrace for us. Only on this condition will we agree to you. If you will be as we are, that every male of you be circumcised."

If this condition is too tough...

"And if you will not listen to us, to be circumcised, then will we take our daughter, and we will be gone."

But the unexpected happened.

Their words pleased Hamor and Shechem. The young man did not delay to do this because he was anxious to have Yaakov's daughter. And he was honored above all the house of his father.

It is amazing that a man will be ready to circumcise himself for a woman he loves, but it is even harder to try to convince an entire city to do so.

Hamor and Shechem, his son, came to the gate of their city and spoke with the men of their city, saying: "These men are peaceable with us. Let them live in the land and trade there for, behold, the land is large enough for them. Let us take their daughters for us for wives and let us give them our daughters. Only on this condition will the men consent to us to live with us, to become one people. Every male among us must be circumcised, as they are.

"Shall not their cattle and their substance and all their

beasts be ours? Only let us consent to them and they will live with us."

And all the people of Shechem listened to and obeyed Hamor and Shechem, his son. Every male was circumcised, all the people of his city.

Of all the days of the pain coming after circumcision, the third is the worst.

On the third day, when they were in pain, two of the sons of Yaakov, Shimon and Levi, Dinah's brothers, each took his sword and came upon the city quietly, and slew all the males. They killed Hamor and Shechem his son by the edge of the sword and took Dinah out of Shechem's house and left.

It wasn't only Shimon and Levi who come to the city...

The sons of Yaakov came upon the dead, and looted the city that defiled their sister. They took their flocks, their herds, their asses, and all that was in the city and that which was in the field. All their wealth, all their little ones and their wives, they took captive and looted all that was in the house.

The revenge is total and terrible. Yaakov is very concerned about the response of the Gentile neighbors.

Yaakov said to Shimon and Levi: "You have put me in danger, to make me repulsive to the inhabitants of the land, even to the Canaanites and the Perizites. While I am very few in number, they will gather themselves together against me and kill me. I shall be destroyed, I and my house."

The brothers respond...

"No one should deal with our sister as a harlot."

Once again, God intervenes.

They journeyed and a fear of God was upon the cities that were around. They did not pursue after the sons of Yaakov.

Now Yaakov goes to meet his father in Be'er Sheva. He leaves behind the smoking city of Shechem and the people remember three issues on which Yaakov leaves his mark.

One, Yaakov might be small in numbers, but nobody should miscalculate his response in case of provocation.

Two, trading with honesty is crucial and cannot be done without proper weights and measures.

Three, there is a piece of land Yaakov purchased in Shechem, waiting for the time to be used as a burial site for his son, Yosef.

In The Time Of
The Judges

Gidon in Shechem

Judges: 8, 9

Shechem is the scene of a unique story about power and people who have no barriers when it comes to domination and honor. The lesson that comes from this story leads us to a very wise saying we can find in the Midrash – "Love work and fear politics."

One of the greatest Judges that Israel has during the time of the Judges is Gidon. He is also known as Yerubbaal because he destroys the idol of Baal in his city. Gidon saves Israel from the hands of Midian and manages to reign 40 years of peace and quiet for the people.

Midian accepted the domination of the Children of Israel and they lifted up their heads no more. And the land had rest forty years in the days of Gidon.

There is always a question after the period of a great leader of who will be able to fill his shoes and maintain his achievements.

In the case of Gidon, the question was even greater because...

Gidon has seventy sons emerging from his loins for he had many wives.

After Gidon dies...

The Children of Israel did not remember the Lord their God, who had delivered them out of the hand of all their enemies on every side.

While the 70 sons of Gidon were not too anxious to rule Israel, the people of Israel did not ask any of them to be the leader, either.

They did not show grace to the house of Yerubbaal, namely Gidon, according to all the goodness which he had shown to Israel.

Of all the wives of Gidon...

His concubine who was in Shechem bore him a son and he called his name Avimelech.

This son was very ambitious.

Avimelech, the son of Yerubbaal, went to Shechem to his mother's brothers and spoke with them and with all the family of the house of his mother's father, saying: "Speak, please in the ears of all the men of Shechem: 'What is better for you, that all the sons of Yerubbaal, who are seventy persons, rule over you, or that one rule over you?' Remember also that I am your bone and your flesh."

This is a typical story of thirst for power and uncontrolled urge for domination because the brothers of his mother, the concubine of Gidon, think about the good positions they will receive from the new king, who is related to them.

Avimelech can count on their eagerness for power to support him to be the king. None of them think about the ingratitude they are paying the family of Gidon who saved them.

And his mother's brothers spoke of him in the ears of all the men of Shechem all these words and their hearts inclined to follow Avimelech for they said: "He is our brother."

And when everyone is sure of his share in power...

They gave him seventy pieces of silver from of the house of Baal Brit.

What passion for power cannot buy, money can.
Avimelech uses it to hire vain and light people.
The rest is bloody and cruel, but simple.
He went to his father's house at Ofrah and killed his brothers, the sons of Yerubbaal, being seventy persons on one stone.
The plan is almost one hundred percent successful...
But Yotam, the youngest son of Yerubbaal, survived for he hid himself.
In Shechem, the spectacular ceremony for the new king starts when...
All the men of Shechem assembled themselves together and all Beit Millo and went and made Avimelech king, by the oak of the pillar that was in Shechem.
In the middle of the party, suddenly the voice of Yotam, coming from Mount Gerizim, hushed the people.
He went and stood on the top of Mount Gerizim and lifted up his voice and cried and said to them: "Listen to me, men of Shechem, and God will listen to you.
The people of Shechem are quite in shock when they see Yotam. They thought all the sons of Gidon were dead. The voice they hear is very disturbing.
Yotam reminds them of a short story.
The trees went to anoint a king over them.
They said to the olive tree: "You reign over us. But the olive tree said to them: "Am I going to leave my richness, seeing that by me they honor God and man and go to hold wave over the trees?"
The trees said to the fig tree: "Come and reign over us."
But the fig tree said to them: "Am I going to leave my sweetness and my good fruit and go to hold wave over the trees?"
The trees said to the grape vine: "Come and reign over us."
The grape vine said to them: "Am I going to leave my wine which cheers God and man and go to wave over the trees?"

When all the trees refuse to take this position, the trees go to the bramble, who has no shade, who has no fruit, who has thorns, and is the first to be consumed with fire in the summertime.

The trees said to the bramble: "Come and reign over us."

The bramble said to the trees: "If in truth you anoint me king over you, then come and take refuge in my shadow. If not, let fire come out of the bramble, and devour the cedars of Lebanon.

The message is clear. Yotam shows the people of Shechem the evil and unjust way they acted.

"Now therefore, if you have dealt truly and uprightly in that you have made Avimelech king and if you have dealt well with Yerubbaal and his house and have done to him according to the deserving of his hands, for my father fought for you and endangered his life and delivered you out of the hand of Midian and you have risen up against my father's house this day and have slain his sons, seventy persons on one stone, and have made Avimelech, the son of his maid servant, king over the men of Shechem, because he is your brother, then you have dealt truly and uprightly with Yerubbaal and with his house this day, so you can rejoice in Avimelech and let him also rejoice in you.

"But if not, let fire come out from Avimelech and devour the men of Shechem and Beit Millo. Let fire come out from the men of Shechem and from Beit Millo and devour Avimelech."

Yotam leaves his message to echo in the air of Shechem and he runs away.

It takes three years for a new atmosphere to build between the people of Shechem and Avimelech. The blood of the 70 sons of Gidon makes the people of Shechem rethink what they have done.

Avimelech was prince over Israel three years. God sent an evil spirit between Avimelech and the men of Shechem. They dealt treacherously with Avimelech so that the violence done to the seventy sons of Yerubbaal might come and that their blood might be laid on Avimelech their brother, who killed them and on the men of Shechem, who strengthened his hands to kill his brothers.

In the beginning, the activity against Avimelech is hidden.

The men of Shechem set an ambush party for him on the tops of the mountains and they robbed all that came along that way by them. It was told to Avimelech.

Later, a man, Gaal ben Eved, dares to say...

"Who is Avimelech and who is Shechem, that we should serve him? Is not he the son of Yerubbaal? And Zevul his officer? Serve you the men of Hamor the father of Shechem. But why should we serve him?

You can tell the man seeks power.

"If these people would accept me as their master, then I would get rid of Avimelech." And he said to Avimelech: "Increase your army and come out."

The mayor of Shechem invites Avimelech...

When Zevul, the ruler of the city, heard the words of Gaal ben Eved, his anger was kindled.

He sent messengers to Avimelech in Tormah, saying: "Behold, Gaal ben Eved and his brothers are coming to Shechem. They will incite the city against you.

So Zevul makes a plan...

"Come at night, you and the people who are with you. Wait in the field. It shall be that in the morning, as soon as the sun is up, you will rise early and set out for the city. When he and the people who are with him come out against you, then you may do to them as you will be able."

Morning comes and Gaal has to act...

Avimelech rose up, and all the people who were with him from the night. They lay in wait against Shechem in four companies. Gaal ben Eved went out and stood in the entrance of the gate of the city. Avimelech rose up and the people that were with him from the ambush.

When Gaal saw the people, he said to Zevul: "People are coming down from the tops of the mountains."

And Zevul said to him: "You see the shadow of the mountains, as if they were men."

Then Gaal spoke again and said: "See the people coming down by the middle of the land, and one company comes by the way of Elon Meonenim."

Zevul's plan works nicely and asks...

"Where is your mouth that you said: 'Who is Avimelech, that we should serve him?' These are the people that you so despise. Please go now and fight them."

Gaal has no choice...

So Gaal went out before the men of Shechem and fought with Avimelech. And Avimelech chased him and he fled before him. There fell many wounded, even at the entrance of the gate.

Gaal, who could not get rid of Avimelech, must leave...

And Zevul sent away Gaal and his brothers so that they should not live in Shechem.

The next morning the story comes to an end.

Avimelech and the companies that were with him rushed forward and stood in the entrance of the gate of the city. The two companies rushed all who were in the field and killed them. Avimelech fought against the city all that day. He took the city and killed the people who were there. He beat down the city and sowed it with salt.

The people of Shechem try to find shelter in the tower of the city.

It was told to Avimelech that all the men of the tower of Shechem were gathered together. Avimelech climbed up to Mount Tzalmon, he and all the people who were with him.

The people who are with Avimelech are not people of big words and long explanations. A personal example is enough...

Avimelech took an axe in his hand and cut down a branch

from the trees and took it up and laid it on his shoulder. He said to the people that were with him: "What you have seen me do, hurry and do exactly as I have done."

All the people did the same and cut down their branches and followed Avimelech and placed them on the hold and set the hold on fire.

Three years ago relations between the people of Shechem and Avimelech looked promising. But now it is clear that they were mistaken and sinful, just as Yotam had said to the people of Shechem.

All the men of the tower of Shechem died, also about a thousand men and women.

Right after Avimelech destroys Shechem, he goes to Tevetz, who also tries to start a revolt against him. While he builds his siege, a woman smashes his head with a piece of stone from the wall.

A certain woman cast an upper millstone on Avimelech's head and broke his skull.

Avimelech calls his servant boy...

"Draw your sword and kill me so that men will not say about me that 'A woman killed him.'"

So his servant...

Thrust him through and he died.

A lesson is learned in the Talmud about this story.

Those who chase honor and respect will never find it because honor and respect will run away from them, but honor will find its way to people who do not seek it.

Thus God repaid the wickedness of Avimelech, which he did to his father by killing his seventy brothers. All the wickedness of the men of Shechem God paid back on their heads and on them came the curse of Yotam the son of Yerubbaal.

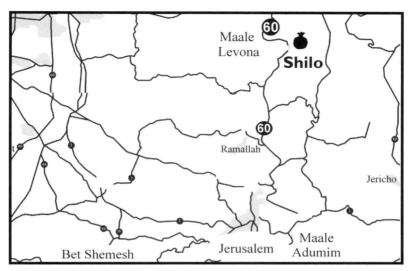

In The Time Of The Judges
Judges: 20, 21

Shilo

In the heart of the land of the tribe Efraim, east to the Road Of The Patriarchs going from Jerusalem to the city of Shechem, are located the ruins of the ancient city of Shilo, the city that hosted the *Mishkan*, built by Moshe in the desert.

The whole congregation of the Children of Israel assembled themselves together at Shilo and erected the Mishkan there. (Yehoshua 18:1)

For 369 years, from the time of Yehoshua until the time of the Prophet Shmuel when the city is conquered and burned by the Philistines, Shilo is the spiritual, national center for the Israelite tribes.

Today, after many years of destruction and desolation, there is a new community in Shilo resettling the mountains, cultivating the land, bringing back the existence of Israel to these landscapes.

Every year on the 15th of the Hebrew month Av, this community celebrates a very unique event, "the holiday of love." This holiday is about matching single young men and women for marriage to make new families in Israel.

The source of this holiday goes back 3,300 years to the time of the Judges when a major crisis between the tribe of Benjamin and all the other of the tribes of Israel took place. This conflict was about the shameful event that happened with the concubine in Giva. *(See the story of Giva.)*

The catastrophic result of the battle between the brothers was that almost the entire tribe of Benjamin perished.

All who fell that day from Benjamin were twenty and five thousand men that drew the sword. All these were men of valor.

The frustration and rage is so intense that...

The men of Israel returned back to the Children of Benjamin and killed them with the edge of the sword, the entire city, the cattle, and all that they found. And all the cities that they found, they set on fire.

Only 600 men from Benjamin survived.

Six hundred men turned and fled toward the wilderness to the rock of Rimmon and they stayed at the rock of Rimmon four months.

These men did not have any wives. They would not marry Gentile women on the one hand and on the other, the people of Israel would not give them their daughters...

The men of Israel had sworn in Mizpah, saying: "None of us shall give his daughter to Benjamin as a wife."

So these men stayed on a rock at Rimmon without women and without the ability to have families.

After the dust of the battle settled, and the size of the horrible damage that infected Benjamin was revealed...

The Children of Israel repented for Benjamin their brother and said: "There is one tribe cut off from Israel this day. How shall we provide wives for those that remain, seeing we have sworn by the Lord that we will not give them from our daughters as wives?"

In order to continue the tribe of Benjamin and still not break the vow which Israel took upon themselves, an original idea was suggested.

They said: "Behold, there is a feast to the Lord, from year to year in Shilo, which is north of Beit El, on the east side of the highway that goes up from Beit El to Shechem, and on the south of Levona."

The Talmud explains that the feast was the festival that marked the opening of the harvest of the vineyards in the valleys around Shilo on the 15th of Av. *(Rashi Shmuel 1: 20,30)*

They commanded the Children of Benjamin, saying: "Go and lie in wait in the vineyards. See if the daughters of Shilo come out to dance in the dances..."

The girls of Israel, dressed in white, used to go down dancing, singing, and harvesting the first grapes.

"Then you will come out of the vineyards and catch for yourself every man his wife from the daughters of Shilo."

One Benjamite is too shy to kidnap a girl for himself, so one of the girls kidnaps him. The name of this man is Shaul, who later becomes the first king of Israel. *(Shmuel 1: 30,20)*

This kind of matching was not the most gentle, but worked. In this way, the tribe of Benjamin could continue and Israel did not break its vow not to *give* its daughters to Benjamin.

The meaning of the name "holiday of love" meant not only love between man and woman, but also referred to the reconciliation between the tribes of Israel. Peace and love dwelled once again among the Israelites when Benjamin is accepted back as one of the twelve tribes of Israel.

The Children of Benjamin did so. They took for themselves wives from the dancers, whom they carried off. They returned to their inheritance and built the cities and settled in them.

Then the Children of Israel departed at that time, every man to his tribe and to his family. They went and returned, every man to his inheritance.

In The Time Of
The Judges

Shilo
The Birth Of Shmuel
Shmuel 1: 1-3

One of the highest and most important moments in a man's life is when he manages to connect with God. Three times every day, Jews strive to make this connection with their prayers.

In Jewish prayer, one of the most important parts is the *Shmona Esray,* 18 requests. This section used to be said silently, from memory. This method of quiet prayer was founded by a barren woman who, during the 20 years that she prayed for a son, would come time after time to the Mishkan in Shilo begging God to answer her. The name of this woman is Hannah and her husband is Elkanah. They were living in the city of Rama.

Today the ruins of Rama lie beneath the Arab village of El-Ram, located north of Jerusalem and south of Beit El.

Now there was a certain man of Ramataim Zophim, of the hill country of Efraim, and his name was Elkanah, the son of Yerucham, the son of Elihu, the son of Tohu, the son of Zuf, an Efraimite. And he had two wives. The name of one was Hannah. The name of the other was Peninnah. Peninnah had children, but Hannah had no children.

This man went up out of his city from year to year to wor-

ship and to sacrifice to the Lord of Hosts in Shilo.

In Shilo, Elkanah would make everyone very happy after the sacrifice...

He gave to Peninnah his wife and to all her sons and her daughters, portions. But to Hannah, he gave a double portion, for he loved Hannah. But the Lord had closed her womb.

Peninnah, Elkanah's other wife, hurt Hannah again and again for having no children.

And her rival bothered her and irritated her, because the Lord had closed her womb. As He did so year by year, when she went up to the House of the Lord, so she irritated her. Therefore she cried and would not eat.

Everyone seems pleased and content, only Hannah is busy with one thought...having a son.

Elkanah, her husband, said to her: "Hannah, why are you crying? Why are you not eating? Why is your heart upset? Am I not better to you than ten sons?"

Hannah realizes that nobody understands her pain...

So Hannah rose up after they had eaten in Shilo, and after they had drunk. Now Eli the Kohen sat on his seat by the door of the sanctuary of the Lord. She

> Elkanah had a very special custom he followed when he would go to the Mishkan in Shilo for the holidays.
>
> On his way with the people of his city, together with his family, he would always choose a different route. As he passed through cities and villages, he encouraged the people, saying, "We are going to the House of God. Join us." The people answered, "Yes, of course, we will." In this way, every year Elkanah would bring more and more people to the Mishkan. This is the meaning of "from year to year" the Tanach uses to describe the custom of Elkanah. *(Tana Devei Eliyahu Raba 8)*

According to the Talmud, Hannah made a kind of threat to God, saying, "look and see," which meant, "if You look at my passion and give me a son, fine, but if You do not, then I will go and be seen with another man to make my husband jealous of me. Then I am going to be taken to the Mishkan and be forced to drink the bitter waters, testing whether I betrayed my husband.

"When I will be found innocent, according to Your Torah, You will have to give me a son, as you have promised to do for a woman who has been falsely accused by her husband. So please do help me." *(Brachot 31)*

was feeling bitter and prayed to the Lord. She wept continuously.

She made a vow and said: "O Master of Legions, if you will look and see the suffering of Your handmaid and remember me, and not forget Your handmaid, but will give to Your handmaid a male child, then I will give him to the Lord, all the days of his life. No razor will come to his head."

Hannah is so deeply engaged in her prayer, she is not aware that...

Eli watches her mouth. Now Hannah, she spoke in her heart. Only her lips moved, but her voice could not be heard.

Seeing all the people around, happily eating and drinking...

Eli thinks she is drunk.

Besides the pain that Hannah bears, now she must deal with the humiliation.

Eli said to her: "How long will you be drunk? Remove the wine from yourself."

Hannah corrects the *Kohen Gadol*, who treats her disrespectfully.

"No, my lord, I am a woman of aggravated spirit. I have drunk neither wine nor strong drink. I poured out my soul before

the Lord.

And about the way I looked...

"Do not consider your handmaid as a wicked woman, for it is out of much grievance and anger that I have spoken until now."

Eli realizes his mistake and says...

"Go in peace and the God of Israel will grant your petition that you have asked of Him."

So she said: "Let your servant find favor in your sight." The woman

The Midrash tells us that Hannah is the first to use the title, "Master of Legions" when she turns to God complaining, "Look at all of these Legions You have here."

She refers to the thousands and thousands of people who come to the Mishkan. "Why cannot I have just one, like them?" She continues saying, "These breasts that I have, why did you give them to me, if not for nursing a baby?" *(Brachot 31)*

went her way, and did eat and her spirit was no longer sad.

Morning comes and everybody leaves for their home...

Elkanah knew Hannah his wife, and the Lord remembered her. And the time came that Hannah conceived and bore a son. She called his name Shmuel, "because I have asked him from the Lord."

And when the next holiday comes and Elkanah and all of his house goes to the House of God...

Hannah did not go up. She said to her husband: "Until the child will be weaned, then I will bring him, that he may appear before the Lord, and there he will stay forever."

Elkanah understands...

"Do what seems good to you. Remain until you have weaned him. Only the Lord will establish His word." So the woman stayed and nursed her son, until she weaned him.

Time passes and little Shmuel grows to be a young boy. His mother does not forget her vow.

She took him up with her, with three bullocks, and one ephah of meal, and a bottle of wine, and brought him to the House of the Lord in Shilo. The child was young.

And when the bullock was slain, the child was brought to Eli.

The sweet moment Hannah was waiting for becomes reality...

And she said: "Oh, my lord, as your soul lives, my lord, I am the woman that stood by you here, praying to the Lord. For this child I prayed. The Lord granted me my petition which I asked from Him. Therefore I have lent him to the Lord. As long as he lives he is lent to the Lord." And he worshipped the Lord there.

Hannah stands before God once again, pouring out her heart, this time for joy and gratitude..

Hannah prayed and said: My heart exults in the Lord. My personality is exalted in the Lord. My mouth is opened wide over my enemies because I rejoice in your salvation.

There is none holy as the Lord, for there is none beside You. Neither is there any rock like our God.

Do not speak too high. Do not let arrogancy come out of

According to the Midrash, the reason Elkanah was blessed with a son like Shmuel, who was known to be as great as both Moshe and Aharon together, is because of the custom Elkanah had every holiday to come with new and large numbers of followers to the House of God in Shilo.

The Midrash says God turned to him saying, "You brought my people to me, so I will give you a son."

Elkanah's son, Shmuel, merited to be the Prophet who anointed the first king of Israel, Shaul, and later David, the greatest king of Israel. *(Tana Devei Eliyahu Raba 8) your mouth for God is a God of knowledge and by Him actions are weighed.*

The bows of the mighty men have broken and they that stumbled are girded with strength.

They that were full of food have hired out themselves for bread and they that were hungry have ceased while the barren have born seven, she that had many children has become miserable.

God kills and revives. He brings down to the grave and brings up. The Lord makes poverty and makes richness. He brings low. He also lifts up.

He raises up the poor out of the dust. He lifts up the needy from the dunghill, to make them sit with princes and inherit the throne of honor for the pillars of the earth are the Lord's, and He has set the world on them.

He will watch the track of His righteous ones, but the wicked shall be silenced in darkness for not by strength shall man prevail.

They that fight with the Lord shall be broken to pieces. Against them will He thunder in heaven. The Lord will judge the ends of the earth and He will give strength to His king and exalt the horn of His anointed.

This is the point where a new chapter in the history of the nation of Israel begins. Shmuel is in Shilo under the shade of the Kohen Gadol, Eli. Soon Shmuel becomes the man who navigates Israel into the era of Kings.

When you stand on the Tel of ancient Shilo, archeologists will point to the estimated location of where the Mishkan once stood. This is the very place were Shmuel spent these years.

The little boy who was brought by his mother...

...grew up and improved both with the Lord and also with men.

In the meantime, Eli turns into an old, heavy, and blind man whose sons do not walk in the path of their father.

The man of God comes to Eli, saying...

"Thus says the Lord: Did I reveal Myself to the house of your father when they were in Egypt in bondage to Pharaoh's house? And did I choose him out of all the tribes of Israel to be My Kohen, to go up to My altar to burn incense, to wear an ephod before Me? And did I give to the house of your father all the offerings of the Children of Israel made by fire?

So why is it that...

"You disgrace My sacrifice and My offering, which I have commanded in My dwelling place.

And why is it that...

"You honored your sons more than Me, to make yourselves fat with the best of all the offerings of Israel My people?"

So...

The Lord, the God of Israel, said: "I said indeed that your house and the house of your father should walk before Me forever," but now the Lord said: "Be it far from Me for, those that honor Me, I will honor, and they that despise Me, shall be disgraced."

And the man of God promises...

"That the days will come that I will cut off your arm and the arm of your father's house, that there shall not be an old man in your house. And you shall behold a rival in My dwelling place in all the good which shall be done to Israel. There shall not be an old man in your house forever.

"Yet I will not cut off every man from My altar, to make your eyes fail, and your heart languish. All the descendants of your house shall die as young men."

This horrible destiny waits for the family of Eli, because he was careless and forgiving when he saw the crimes of his sons. The man of God concludes his terrifying message...

"And this shall be the sign to you, that Hophni and Pinchas, in one day, they shall die, both of them."

Eli, the Kohen Gadol, did not change his attitude towards his sons, despite of the words from the man of God, so God seeks another channel to pass on his message.

"And I will raise up a faithful Kohen for Me, who will do according to that which is in My heart and in My mind. I will build him a loyal house. He shall walk before My anointed forever."

Although Shmuel may be young in the eyes of the people around him, in the eyes of God, he is ready to take on

According to the Talmud, during the time of the great Rabbi Yochanan ben Zackai, there was a family of Kohanim in Jerusalem who died very young. "What can be done for us? We all die before becoming 18 years old," they asked of the great Rabbi.

"Are you from the family of Eli the Kohen Gadol?"

"Yes we are," they said.

So Rabbi Yochanan ben Zackai told them, "Go and spread charity. That is the only way you can save yourself from your family's curse and live to an old age." (*Yevamot 105, p1*)

his shoulders the burden of the leadership of Israel.

And the first experience of talking to God happens in a quite surprising way.

Shmuel was lying in the Temple of the Lord, where the Ark of God was. The Lord called Shmuel and He said: "Here I am."

Shmuel thinks, "Who can call me. It must be Eli."

And he ran to Eli and said: "Here I am for you called me."

And he said: "I did not call. Go and lie back down."

And the same thing happened a second time.

And the Lord called yet again Shmuel. And Shmuel arose and went to Eli and said: "Here I am. Did you call me?"

And he answered: "I did not call, my son. Go back and lie down."

Shmuel did not yet know the Lord and the word of the Lord was not yet revealed to him.

And when it happened a third time...

And the Lord called Shmuel again the third time. He arose and went to Eli and said: "Here I am for you did call me."

It was clear...

And Eli understood that the Lord was calling the child.

And in a one sentence course, Eli prepares Shmuel to be the Prophet.

"Go, lay down and it shall be, if you are called, you shall say: 'Speak Lord, for Your servant hears.'"

Shmuel returns to his bed, waiting for God to call his name again.

The Lord came and stood, and called as at other times: "Shmuel, Shmuel." Then Shmuel said: "Speak for Your servant hears."

Without any preparations, God turns to the young man, Shmuel, and describes the horrible destiny awaiting the family of Eli, who abused the name of God and His shrine.

The Lord said to Shmuel: "Behold, I will do a thing in Israel, that when anyone hears about it, both of the ears of everyone that hears it, shall ring.

"On that day, I will perform against Eli all that I have spoken concerning his house, from the beginning to the end. I have told him that I will judge his house forever, for the sin that he knew that his sons brought as a curse upon themselves, and he did not rebuke them. Therefore I have sworn to the house of Eli that the sins of Eli's house shall not be atoned for with sacrifice or offering forever."

From this moment, Shmuel gets the authorization by God to be the man who will guide Israel.

In The Time Of
The Judges

Shilo
The Mishkan Moves
Shmuel 1: 4

Shortly after Shmuel experiences the first prophecy, there is a war between the Israelites and the Philistines. The battle takes place in the fields of Evan HaEzer, which is east of the springs of the Yarkon River, today the community of Rosh Ha'Ayan.

The Israelites know that difficulties in the battlefield can be solved by bringing the Ark of the Covenant, so they have no reason to doubt that the presence of the Ark will help overcome the enemy this time too.

When the people came into the camp, the elders of Israel said: "Why did the Lord defeat us today before the Philistines? Let us get the Ark of the Covenant of the Lord out of Shilo to us so that He may be among us and save us out of the hand of our enemies."

Shmuel, as a young man, is powerless to stop the people from taking the Ark. Eli, on the other hand, is too old and no one will listen to him.

So the people sent to Shilo and they brought the Ark of the Covenant of the Lord of Hosts, who sits on the Cherubim. The two sons of Eli, Hophni and Pinchas, were there with the Ark of the Covenant of God.

But the arrival of the Ark to Evan HaEzer did not help...

The Philistines fought and Israel was defeated. They fled, every man to his tent, and there was a very great slaughter. There fell of Israel, thirty thousand soldiers.

And the worst happens when...

The Ark of God was taken and the two sons of Eli, Hophni and Pinchas, were slain.

From the battlefield, a man flees.

A man from Benjamin ran out from the battle and came to Shilo the same day with his clothes rent and with earth upon his head.

As he enters Shilo, people listen to what happened...

All the city cried out.

Eli heard the cry and asked...

"What is all this noise of the crowd?"

A soldier came to Eli reporting...

"I am the one who fled from the battlefield. Israel fled before the Philistines and there has been a great slaughter among the people. Your two sons, Hophni and Pinchas, are dead. The Ark of God has been taken."

Eli cannot bear the list of terrible events, concluding with the loss of the Ark of the Covenant.

He fell off his seat backward by the side of the gate. His neck broke and he died, for he was an old man, and heavy. He had judged Israel forty years.

This list of catastrophes for the family of Eli continues when...

His daughter-in-law, Pinchas' wife, who was pregnant, heard that the Ark of God had been taken, and that her father-in-law and her husband were dead, crouched down and gave birth for her pains came suddenly.

As she gives birth, she dies.

About the time of her death, the women that stood by her said to her: "Fear not for you have brought forth a son." But she did not answer and she did not care.

With all the shame, the pain, and the agony of the day, there is only one thing left to do.

She named the child Ekavod, saying: "The glory has departed from Israel," because the Ark of God has been taken and because of the death of her father-in-law and her husband.

Not long after, the victorious army of the Philistines marches to Shilo. The people must flee before the Philistines burn the city to ash.

At this point, the Ark of the Covenant is on its way to the Philistine city of Gaza.

In order to save the Mishkan, the Israelites dismantle it and move it to a safer city. For 52 years, the House of God moves from city to city, until David brings it to Jerusalem.

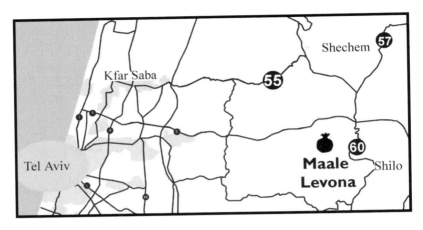

In The Time Of The Judges
Judges: 17

Maale Levona

Near Shilo, the highway to Shechem descends to the beautiful Levona Valley. West of this valley, on a slope of the mountain, there is an Arab village that preserves the name of a city once called Levona. East of the road meandering down to the valley, there is a mountain isolated from all sides by deep valleys. Today on top of this mountain, there is the Jewish community of Maale Levona.

The view that you see from the top of Maale Levona is breathtaking. To the west, you can see the entire coast of Israel, including the Mediterranean Sea. To the north, the whole land of Efraim and the Shomron can be seen, including the mountains of Gerizim and Aval, and the city of Shechem. And on very special clear days, very far north, the snow-capped Mount Herman can be seen.

The name Levona refers to a spice found in the area that was used as part of the Temple's sacrificial service which was known as the *Ketoret*.

On the Maale Levona mountain, the Book of Judges records a story about Michayahu, who steals 1100 pieces of silver from his mother.

When he hears her cursing the thief, he confesses.

"The eleven hundred pieces of silver that were taken from you, about which you did utter a curse, and did also speak in my ears, behold, the silver is with me. I took it."

Like a good mother, her response is...

"Blessed be my son of the Lord."

Then she decides to take the money and do something "good" with it.

"I truly dedicate the silver to the Lord from my hand for my son, to make a graven image and a molten image."

So she takes 200 pieces of silver and gives it to the silversmith. From it, he makes a sculpture that looks just like the golden calf the Israelites made at Mount Sinai.

Now this sculpture needs a nice room to sit in and someone to serve it.

And the man Micha had a house of God, and he made an ephod, and teraphim, and consecrated one of his sons, who became his priest.

The Tanach adds a remark to the story that helps us understand the mood of the people.

In those days there was no king in Israel. Every man did that which was right in his own eyes.

From this story, we realize that in the same place, the same area, and for the same people, there are two sites of worship. One in Shilo, to God, which as we know, prohibits idols. And the other, three miles west, where people were worshiping idols. There were even some Israelites, who either before or after going to the House of God in Shilo, would pay a visit to the idol's site in the house of Micha.

Strangely, we learn from the Talmud that the smoke coming from the altar of the idol of Micha would actually mix with the smoke coming from God's altar in Shilo. *(Sanhedrin 103)*

As we said...

In those days there was no king in Israel. Every man did that which was right in his own eyes.

Micha is bothered by something that he thinks is a problem - the man serving his idol is not a real Kohen from the tribe of Levi, as it was in the Mishkan in Shilo. So Micha finds a solution, thanks to another source of income he has.

On the mountain of Levona, Micha operates a small guest house where travelers stay the night.

And there was a young man out of Beit Lechem in Yehuda – in the family of Yehuda – who was a Levite. The man departed out of the city, out of Beit Lechem in Yehuda, to look where he could find a place to live. He came to the hill country of Efraim, to the house of Micha, as he journeyed.

Micha meets the young man in his guest house and the discussion goes as follows...

Micha said to him: "Where do you come from?"

And he said to him: "I am a Levite of Beit Lechem in Yehuda, and I go to see where I may find a place to live."

Not a man to miss this opportunity...

Micha said to him: "Dwell with me and be to me a father and a Kohen."

And for the salary...

"I will give you ten pieces of silver by the year, a suit of clothes, and your food."

So the Levite went in.

Never before, or after, does the Tanach gives us the details of an interaction between a worker and his boss the way it appears in this story. It looks like both of them, Micha and the young Levite, are getting along very well...

The Levite was content to dwell with the man. The young man was to him as one of his sons.

Micha consecrated the Levite. The young man became his Kohen and was in the house of Micha. The Levite is happy to have a place to live that provides all his needs. And Micha is very happy because he thinks that now his pagan business will flourish, thanks to the Levite.

Then Micha said: "Now I know that the Lord will do good for me, seeing I have a Levite as my Kohen."

That is what the Tanach meant when it states...

In those days there was no king in Israel. Every man did that which was right in his own eyes.

According to the Talmud, the Levite's full name is Yehonatan, son of Gershom, son of Menashe.

In the Hebrew script of the Tanach, the name Menashe is written with the letter *nun* above the rest of the letters. From this, the Talmud hints that there is something special about the lineage of Yehonatan.

We learn that Yehonatan is really the grandson of Moshe, the very Moshe who takes the Children of Israel out of Egypt and gives them the Torah on Mount Sinai.

If you take the letter *nun* out of the script, the name Moshe will appear. Since Menashe was known to be the worst idol-worshiping king in Jerusalem, the Talmud says that Yehonatan's full name is written this way to save Moshe the embarrassment that his grandson serves idols.

(Bava Batra p109)

Menashe was twelve years old when he began to reign. He did that which was evil in the sight of the Lord, abominations of the nations, whom the Lord cast out before the Children of Israel. He built again the high places which Hezekiah his father had destroyed. He built up altars for Baal and made an Asherah, as did Achav, king of Israel and worshipped the stars of the sky and served them. (Kings 2: 21)

It is Moshe who teaches in the Torah that idol worship must be uprooted. In the Torah *(Shemot: 20)*, the second commandment written is...

You shall have no other gods before Me.

You shall not make to yourself a graven image, nor any manner of likeness, of anything that is in heaven above, or that is in the earth beneath, or that is in the water under the earth.

You shall not bow down to them, nor serve them, for I the Lord your God am a jealous God, visiting the iniquity of the fathers upon the children to the third and fourth generation of them that hate Me.

In The Time Of
The Judges

Maale Levona
All Because Of A Fly
Judges: 19

*A*nd it came to pass in those days, when there was no king
in Israel...
When the Tanach starts a story with this opening, it
means that the story is not a simple one.

*There was a certain Levite living on the far side of the hill
country of Efraim, who took to him a concubine out of Beit Lechem
in Yehuda.*

According to the Talmud, the Levite is Yehonatan who
takes a concubine for himself from his city, Beit Lechem.

*His concubine acted as the harlot against him and left him
for her father's house in Beit Lechem in Yehuda and was there
four months.*

The Talmud explains *(Gitin 6)* that the phrase *acted as
the harlot against him,* unlike what you would think, means
that he found a fly in the soup that she was cooking for him.
The fly in his soup made Yehonatan so outraged that his
concubine became terrified and ran away to her father's house
in Beit Lechem.

Yehonatan must have been a bad-tempered person because it took him quite a while to cool off.

After four months...

Her husband arose, and went after her, to speak nicely to her, to bring her back.

The rest of the story of what happened to the concubine on the way back home to Maale Levona can be found in the story of the city of Giva. This incident is considered to be one of the most horrible events that happened to Israel, involving bloodshed, adultery, and paganism.

In the days of the Tanach, a woman who could not get herself a decent husband in a proper marriage, hoped to be at least a concubine. She would be a woman with few legal rights and low social status.

The concubine's husband would give her financial support, defend her, and most importantly, give her a child who would support her in her old age.

Although the status of this woman was lower and her legal rights were less than a regular wife, this woman belonged to the man and no one else was allowed to be with her.

In the Talmudic discussion of *Bameh Madlekeen,* (What to light with?) there is a lesson to be learned about dealing with tense moments. The discussion refers to the kinds of oils a Jewish person can use to light Shabbat candles.

At the end of the discussion, the Talmud says that there are three things a Jewish person should say before the time of Shabbat begins. "Have you tithed? Have you made the eruv? and Light the Shabbat candles!" These three things, according to the Talmud, must be said in a quiet, calm way.

The answer of the Talmud to the question about why these very three things must be said in a quiet, calm way is because the moments before Shabbat enters are often very tense since everything is not always ready for Shabbat and the pressure can be very high.

At this point, instead of losing control, the man should turn quietly, calmly to his family and finalize the works for Shabbat by setting the tithes, finishing the *eruv* and getting the candles ready to be lit.

The Talmud says a man should never allow fear to enter his house the way Yehonatan frightened his concubine. Fearfulness in a house can lead to three horrible events – bloodshed, adultery, and paganism – like what happened to Israel – all because of a fly in Yehonatan's soup in Maale Levona.

In The Time Of
The Judges

Maale Levona
Trouble In The Guest House
Judges: 18

When the Tanach tells the story of the tribe of Dan heading north to find a new land to live in, leaving their coastal home behind, Maale Levona finds that it has a very important place in the saga of Dan's relocation.

The reason the whole tribe of Dan moves north, abandoning their lifestyle, their fields, their possessions – everything – stems from the death of Shimshon by the Philistines in Gaza. The people of Dan are afraid of the revenge that the Philistines are going to take upon them because of Shimshon's exploits. And they know that none of the Israelite tribes will come to help them against the Philistines, because...

In those days there was no king in Israel. In those days the tribe of Dan sought an inheritance to dwell in.

In order to find a nice quiet piece of land for the whole tribe, five men from the best of the tribe of Dan are sent to look for this land.

The Children of Dan sent from their family five men from their whole number, men of valor, from Zorah, and from Eshtaol, to spy out the land, and to search it. They said to them: "Go, search the land."

These five men make their way along the highway that we know as the Road Of The Patriarchs and arrive to lodge in Maale Levona. They stay the night in the guest house of Micha.

They came to the hill country of Efraim, to the house of Micha, and lodged there.

And now the Tanach describes something that is amazing. *Only by voice*, these five men recognize Yehonatan, the young man serving the idol of Micha.

When they were by the house of Micha, they knew the voice of the young man, the Levite.

How could this be? How could these five men, who come from Dan, recognize, only by voice, a man who is originally from Beit Lechem, and now working for Micha in Maale Levona?

The Talmud gives a hint. *(Bava Batra 91)* We learn that the Danite Manoach, who is the father of Shimshon, is married to the niece of Boaz, the Judge from Beit Lechem-Yehuda. This means that the families of Manoach and Boaz are related, which gives a reason for someone from the tribe of Dan to be associated with someone from the tribe of Yehuda.

It is natural for families to visit each other. So this is how the family of Manoach has reason to be in Beit Lechem and be familiar with the young man, Yehonatan the Levite from Beit Lechem. As a Levite, Yehonatan would often sing in public events, so his voice was well-known and the five men could recognize his voice, before seeing his face.

From this, we understand that the five men from Dan must have been a part of the family of Manoach. Could these five men have been younger brothers of Shimshon that we never knew about?

And they turned and said to him: "Who brought you here? And what are you doing in this place? And what do you have here?"

These questions the five men ask Yehonatan more than refer to the fact that they know him. They are wondering how he can be of help to them.

Yehonatan explains...

"Such and such has Micha done for me. He has hired me and I have become his Kohen."

We understand from Yehonatan's answer that the five men know his family lineage very well. They want to know how it is that the grandson of Moshe is worshipping idols.

When Yehonatan answers, "Such and such has Micha done for me," it means – "It's only a job. I'm doing it only for the money. I don't really believe in the worship of idols."

Then what do these five men do? They ask Yehonatan to inquire to God about *their* mission.

"Ask counsel, please, of God, that we may know whether our way which we are going shall be prosperous."

And Yehonatan says...

"Go in peace. Before the Lord is your way where you go."

The five men leave, heading north...

They came to Laish and saw the people that were there, how they dwelled in security, after the manner of the Zidonians, quiet and secure. There was none in the land, possessing authority, that might put them to shame in anything, and they were far from the Zidonians, and had no dealings with any man.

It looks like the search for a new home is over.

And they came to their brothers to Zorah and Eshtaol. Their brothers asked them: "What did you see?" They said: "Arise, and let us go up against them. We have seen the land and it is very good. Why are you still? Do not be lazy to go and to enter in to possess the land."

The five men are convinced about the good of the land and they try to convince their brothers that it is a good decision.

"When you go, you shall come to a people secure. The land is large. God has given it into your hand, a place where there is no

want. It has everything that is in the earth."

A convoy of people from Dan starts moving north, with a heavy military escort.

They journeyed from there, from the family of the Dan, out of Zorah and out of Eshtaol, six hundred men girt with weapons of war.

Once again, the road used for the convey is the Road Of The Patriarchs. When the people of Dan arrive at Maale Levona...

They came to the house of Micha.

And the five men remember Yehonatan and his idols, who blessed their way, the first time they went north...

The five men that went to spy out the country of Laish said to their brothers: "Do you know that there is in these houses an ephod, and teraphim, and a graven image, and a molten image?"

At this point, the people of Dan need spiritual support. They reason that if it is not going to be good, it is not going to be bad to have the spiritual support of the Levite and his idols.

They came to the house of the young man the Levite, to the house of Micha, and asked him of his welfare.

We can understand the meaning of this question when...

The six hundred men girt with their weapons of war, who were of the Children of Dan, stood by the entrance of the gate.

Meanwhile...

The five men that went to spy out the land went up and came in and took the graven image, the ephod, the teraphim, and the molten image. The Kohen stood by the entrance of the gate with the six hundred men girt with weapons of war.

When these men went into Micha's house and fetched the graven image of the ephod, the teraphim, and the molten image...

Yehonatan the Levite asks...

"What are you doing?"

The answer is very clear.

"Hold your peace. Lay your hand on your mouth and go with us and be to us a father and a Kohen. Is it better for you to be a Kohen to the house of one man or to be a Kohen to a tribe and a family in Israel?"

This seems like Yehonatan has just been offered a proposal that he cannot refuse. We know that Yehonatan never refused a good business proposal, so...

The Kohen's heart was glad. He took the ephod, the teraphim, the graven image, and went in the midst of the people.

Yehonatan was happy with the new job, besides, he had no other choice.

And now the people of Dan try to leave quietly.

So they turned and departed and put the little ones and the cattle and the goods before them. When they were a good way from the house of Micha...

Micha wakes up and starts to chase them.

The men that were in the houses near to Micha's house were gathered together and overtook the Children of Dan. They cried to the Children of Dan.

The 600 men turn back, surprisingly asking...

"What happened to you, that you come with such a company?"

Micha tries to explain...

"You have taken away my god which I made and the Kohen. What more do I have now? How do you ask me: 'What's bothering you'"

The people of Dan try to make Micha understand that he must be logical under these circumstances...

"Let not your voice be heard among us, or else angry fellows will fall upon you, and you will lose your life, with the lives of your household."

Obviously Micha has no other choice but to be logical...

So the Children of Dan went their way. When Micha saw that they were too strong for him, he turned and went back to his house.

From this point, Yehonatan ben Gershom has a job for himself and his descendants..

The Children of Dan set up for themselves the graven image. Yehonatan, the son of Gershom, the son of Menashe, he and his sons were Kohanim to the tribe of the Dan until the day of the captivity of the land.

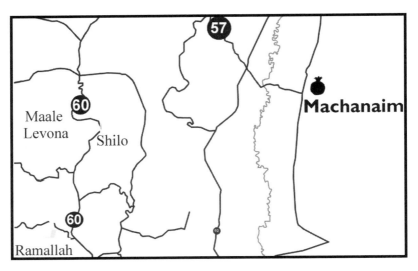

In The Time Of David
Shmuel 2: 17, 18

Machanaim

One of the most beautiful trees in the Israeli forest is the *kotlav*. This tree bears red fruits in the summertime and has an absolutely red trunk. The branches of these trees look like they are bleeding, because of their color.

The meaning of the name kotlav in Hebrew, *kottel av*, is killing a father. This stems from a legend about a son who killed his father under this tree and that because the blood of the father spilled on the tree, he painted the tree red.

This legend refers to an event described in the Tanach that happened to King David when his son, Avshalom, tries to kill him.

The Tanach describes David, who tries to avoid confrontation with his son, so much so that he goes into exile, leaving behind his city Jerusalem...

And David arrived to Machanaim

At this point David and his men are refugees looking for shelter, running away from Avshalom's army.

But Avshalom does not wait. After he enters Jerusalem, he gets ready for war. He leaves Jerusalem, chasing his father.

Avshalom passed over the Jordan, he and all the men of Israel with him.

Now the Tanach describes the people loyal to David. These people, who by being around David, risk their lives because Avshalom, after killing his father, will not be merciful and will kill all the people who are now with David. But still there are those good people who support David in everything he does.

And it happened when David arrived to Machanaim, that Shobi, the son of Nachash of Rabbah of the Children of Ammon, and Machir, the son of Ammiel of Lodevar, and Barzillai, the Giladite of Rogelim, brought beds, basins, earthen vessels, wheat, barley, meal, parched corn, beans, lentils, parched pulse, honey, curd, sheep, and cheese of kine for David and for the people that were with him to eat. For they said: "The people are hungry and faint, and thirsty, in the wilderness."

It is clear that very soon these people will have to fight Avshalom and his army. No one guarantees them an easy victory. They may lose the battle. They may be killed and lose their homes and families. But these people are absolutely devoted to their King. They are ready to do anything for him. On the very day of the battle between Avshalom's army and the people supporting David...

David numbered the people that were with him, and set captains of thousands and captains of hundreds over them.

The people are divided into three units.

David sent forth the people, a third under the hand of Yoav, and a third under the hand of Avishai the son of Zeruiah, Yoav's brother, and a third under the hand of Ittai the Gittite.

The option of David joining his men has been rejected immediately by his supporters...

The people said: "You shall not go forth for if we flee away they will not care about us. Neither if half of us die, will they care about us. But you are worth ten thousand of us. Therefore, it is better that you be ready to help us from the city."

In front of everybody, David turns to Yoav and the people saying...

"Be gentle, for my sake, with the young boy, Avshalom."

A short while later the two armies confront each other.

The battle was in the forest of Efraim.

Something quite unusual happens. Avshalom's people are beaten by David's supporters, thanks to the forest.

The people of Israel were defeated there by the servants of David. There was a great slaughter there that day of twenty thousand men. The battle there was spread over the face of all the country and the forest consumed more people that day than the sword consumed.

Avshalom himself realizes the forest is also fighting against him when...

Avshalom was riding on his mule and the mule went under the thick boughs of a great terebinth and his head caught hold of the terebinth. He was taken up between the heaven and the earth. The mule that was under him went on.

Picture this man, who managed to lead and gather so many of the people of Israel to join him to kill King David – his father – swinging helpless, hanging by his hair from a tree. It is no less than unbelievable.

The Talmud clarifies the reason Avshalom hangs by his hair.

Avshalom is a very handsome man.

Now in all Israel there was none to be so much praised as Avshalom for his beauty, from the sole of his foot to the crown of his head. There was no blemish in him. And when he shaved his head – now it was at every year's end that he barbered it because the hair was heavy on him. Therefore he groomed it. He weighed the hair of his head at two hundred shekels, after the king's weight. (Shmuel 2: 14; 25, 26)

Avshalom used his attractive appearance as a tool to manipulate and control the people of Israel. Now his hair is being used, measure for measure, to hang him on a tree.

Word spread quickly of Avshalom hanging from the tree.

Yoav, who loses no time and despite the warning of the king to...

"Be gentle, for my sake, with the young boy, Avshalom."
Yoav...

...took three darts in his hand and thrust them through the heart of Avshalom while he was still alive in the midst of the terebinth.

Why was Avshalom struck in the heart with three darts? The Talmud tells us that the three darts are, measure for measure, for the three hearts Avshalom betrays. *(Sota 9)*

First Avshalom steals his father's heart, when he tricks him into writing a letter for the people to help him, though he is really planning to use the letter to turn the people against his father.

The second heart he steals is the heart of the elders of Israel by using his father's letter deceptively.

The third heart he steals is the heart of the common people of Israel. When the people are about to be judged by King David, Avshalom tells them that they will not be treated justly and only if he were the judge, would they receive justice.

When any man had a suit which should come to the king for judgment, Avshalom said to him: "See, your matters are good and right, but there is no man authorized by the king to hear you. If I were judge in the land, every man who had any suit or cause might come to me and I would do him justice!"

So Avshalom stole the hearts of the men of Israel.
(Shmuel 2:15)

Right afterwards...

Ten young men that carried Yoav's armor compassed about and smote Avshalom, and killed him.

The Talmud says that the ten young men who kill Avshalom come as measure for measure for what Avshalom did with David's ten concubines. *(Sota 9)*

So they spread Avshalom a tent on the top of the house and Avshalom went into his father's concubines in the sight of all Israel. (Shmuel 2: 16; 22)

After Avshalom is dead, Yoav...

...blew the shofar and the people returned from chasing after Israel for Yoav spared the lives of the people.

The forest of Efraim is located on the eastern side of the Jordan River not so far from the Adam Bridge, which is used today to cross the Jordan River into Jordan. As you travel along the Jordan Valley road today, you see that the forest that used to be here has disappeared. The whole landscape looks desolate, little here, little there, although small farms growing vegetables dot the area.

According to the description in the Tanach, a high hill of rocks has accumulated on the place where the body of Avshalom was thrown.

And they took Avshalom and cast him into the great pit in the forest and raised over him a very great heap of stones.

I wonder where it is.

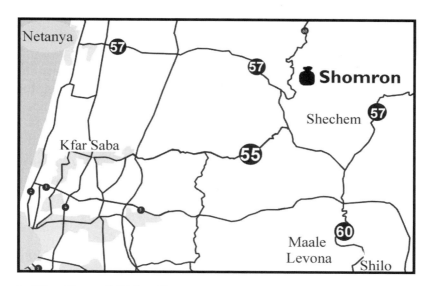

In The Time Of The Kings

Shomron

Kings 1: 16, 20

One of the ways that kings would leave their mark on history was to build a new capital city. And the Israelite King Omri was no different. After taking the crown from Tivni ben Genat, Omri finds the capital, Tirtza, unsuitable for him, so...

He bought the hill Shomron from Shemer for two talents of silver. He built on the hill and called the name of the city which he built, after the name of Shemer, the owner of the hill, Shomron.

Omri was not a king who followed in the ways of God.

Omri did that

According to the Talmud, even though Omri was a pagan king, he would still enjoy *Olam Haba, (the next world)* for the simple reason that he established a new city in Israel. *(Sanhedrin 102)*

which was evil in the sight of the Lord. He dealt wickedly with all that were before him. He walked in the ways of Yerovam, the son of Nevat and in his sins where he caused Israel to sin, to provoke the Lord, the God of Israel, with their vanities.

When Omri dies, his son Achav takes over the position of king of Israel. It looks like there is a new horizon coming for the ten tribes of Israel. The new king seems like a brilliant leader, smart and strong, capable to bring Israel to new heights.

But then...

He took Ezevel, the daughter of Etbaal, king of the Zidonians as his wife.

According to the Talmud, these are the days when Achav's friend, Hiel from Beit El goes down to the Jordan Valley to build a new city on the ruins of Jericho.
(Sanhedrin 10)

From the influence of the new bride...

He went to serve Baal, and worship him. He built an altar for Baal in the house of Baal, which he had built in Shomron. Achav made the Asherah. Achav did more to provoke the Lord, the God of Israel, than all the kings of Israel that were before him.

It goes by tradition... When Israel forsakes God... Enemies arrive at the gate.

And Ben Hadad, the king of Aram, gathered all his staff together. There were thirty and two kings with him, and horses and chariots. He went up and besieged Shomron, and fought against it.

And Aram, the northern neighbor of Israel, also comes for an unfriendly visit, while Shomron, which is not yet seven years old, is still under siege by Ben Hadad.

And he sent messengers to Achav, king of Israel, into the city and said to him: "Thus said Ben Hadad: 'Your silver and your gold is mine. Your wives and your good children are also mine.'"

Achav, who sees the huge army, built of 32 kings surrounding Shomron, understands that there is no hope to resist, so...

The king of Israel answered and said: "It is according to what you said my lord, O king: I am yours and all that I have."

Once again Ben Hadad sends the messengers, saying not only that...

"You will give me your silver and your gold and your wives and your children."

But far more than this...

"I will send my servants to you tomorrow about this time, and they shall search your house and the houses of your servants. It shall be that whatever is pleasant in your eyes, they shall put it in their hand and take it away."

> "Whatever is pleasant in your eyes" means the Torah.
>
> Achav is willing to accept any condition of Ben Hadad, except for giving him the Torah.
>
> *(Shemot Raba 3:8)*

Then Achav calls the elders of the land and says...

"Please note and see how this man seeks evil. He sent for my wives and for my children and for my silver and for my gold. I did not refuse him."

The elders support Achav, who say...

"Do not listen and do not consent."

And so Achav answers Ben Hadad.

"Tell my lord the king, 'All that you did send for your servant the first time, I will do, but this thing, I will not do.'"

It looks strange. Achav, the man who will worship any kind of idol, suddenly is willing to give up everything and put himself into extreme danger and high risk because he refuses to give the Torah, which anyway, he does not follow. Achav's behavior is something that can help us understand the personality of the Israelite king. Achav is a proud nationalist Israelite. He may live a pagan life and ignore Jewish laws, but Israelite symbols are precious in his eyes and he will not give them up. If necessary, he is ready to die for them.

When Ben Hadad hears the answer, he gets angry...

"So will help me the gods. If the dust of Shomron shall be

enough for the number of the people that accompany me."

Achav responds disrespectfully...

"Tell him, a man who wears a sword should not speak like he is already victorious in the battle."

Ben Hadad, assured of his success, drinks together with the other kings in his tent. But when he hears Achav's answer...

He said to his servants: "Start the siege." And they got themselves ready for the siege against the city.

Achav sees the soldiers of Aram getting ready for action. And we can imagine what passes through his head. A city, which his father started, just seven years ago, is about to be destroyed, burned and turned to ash, when suddenly...

A Prophet came near to Achav, king of Israel, and said: "Thus says the Lord: 'Have you seen all this great multitude? Behold, I will deliver it into your hand this day and you shall know that I am the Lord.'"

Achav looks at the Prophet, asking who can stop this crowd. I have nobody capable to block this huge army.

"By whom?"

And the Prophet pointed...

"By the young men of the princes of the provinces."

It is more than absurd to think that these boys, the princes of the provinces, will be able to fight the huge army, but Achav has no other choice.

He numbered the young men of the princes of the provinces. They were two

> The 232 cities were paying taxes to Achav. In order to make sure that these cities would not revolt against him, he takes the princes from the cities to live with him in Shomron. These princes, who are introduced to Judaism and the God of Israel, become righteous people. *(Shemot Raba 3:8)*

hundred and thirty-two. After them, he numbered all the people, even all the Children of Israel, being seven thousand.

Achav, even under these poor conditions, is willing to fight.

And the young men of the princes of the provinces went out first. Ben Hadad sent out and they told him, saying: "There are men who come out from Shomron."

Ben Hadad, very drunk, gets the report of people coming out of the city. He says...

"If they come out for peace, take them alive. If they come out for war, take them alive."

But the unexpected happens.

They slew everyone. The people of Aram fled and Israel pursued them. Ben Hadad, the king of Aram, escaped on a horse with horsemen.

Achav, with very few people, led by 232 princes, manages to defeat the huge army of Aram and liberate the city of Shomron from almost total devastation.

Achav's victory, which can only be described as a miracle, happens because of two reasons. One, Achav would not give up the Torah and is ready to die for it. The other, because the 232 righteous princes who grew up in the house of Achav became believers in God.

But Achav still does not repent and continues to be pagan. Unfortunately because of paganism and his refusal to follow God, the dynasty of Achav is wiped out from the world.

Because the other kings of Israel are no better than Achav, the kingdom of the ten tribes falls into the hands of Sanheriv, the king of Ashur, who exiles the people. Ever since, these are known as the *ten lost tribes.* Sanheriv's war journey winds up destroying all the cities of Israel and its capital, Shomron.

During the time of King Herod, the name Shomron is changed to Sebastia, after the name of the Roman Caesar.

Today, the ruins of Shomron are near the new Jewish settlement of Shavay Shomron, referring to Israel's return to their Land, as the Prophet Yirmiyahu prophesied.

"I have loved you with an everlasting love. Therefore I have extended kindness to you. Again will I build you and you will be built, O maiden of Israel. Again you will be adorned with your drums, and will go forth in the dances of merrymakers. Again you will plant vineyards on the mountains of Shomron. The planters will plant and redeem." (Yirmiyahu: 31;1-5)

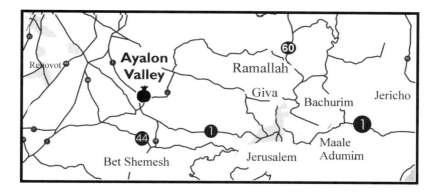

In The Time Of The Judges
Yehoshua: 9, 10

The Ayalon Valley

The area that comprises the southern coast of Israel starts in the east at the footsteps of the mountains of Yehuda and extends west to the Mediterranean Sea. Geographically, the landscape of this area is comprised mostly of sandy low hills. In the valleys among the hills, the area is dotted with small lakes that turn into swamps in the summertime.

In the time of the *Tanach*, Yehoshua ben Nun leads the tribes of Israel into the Land to conquer and settle. During one of the battles in the Valley of Ayalon, an extraordinary event takes place. Ayalon is the wide open valley that you enter as you leave Jerusalem heading to the coast.

When the inhabitants of Givon heard what Yehoshua had done to Jericho and to Ai, they acted cunningly.

Knowing the destiny of the inhabitants of the land of Canaan, that they will be killed by the hand of Yehoshua, the Givonites are terrified.

They went and made as if they were ambassadors, and took old sacks upon their asses, and wine skins, worn and rent and patched up. They tried to fool Yehoshua by looking poor and miserable, and that they were not a part of the Canaanite nation.

They went to Yehoshua in the camp at Gilgal, and said to him, and to the men of Israel: "We are from a far country. Now make a covenant with us."

Yehoshua looks at them and has mercy on them. He gives them the covenant, something he would not have done if he had consulted with God.

Yehoshua did not ask counsel at the mouth of the Lord. Yehoshua made peace with them, and made a covenant with them, to let them live. The princes of the congregation swore to them.

It did not take long for the truth to come out.

It came to pass at the end of three days after they had made a covenant with them, that they heard that they were their neighbors, and that they dwelled among them.

And now that the Israelites discover that they have been fooled, there is a lot of anger and frustration for being so easily deceived by the Givonites, but they say...

"We have sworn to them by the Lord, the God of Israel. Therefore we may not touch them. This we will do to them, and let them live, or else wrath be upon us, because of the oath which we swore to them."

Yehoshua curses the Givonites for misleading him. But, instead of killing them, he makes them the servants of Israel.

And Yehoshua made them that day hewers of wood and drawers of water.

At the same time, the Givonites have also betrayed the military alliance that they made with the other cities of Canaan.

Givon was a great city, as one of the royal cities, and it was greater than Ai. All the men there were mighty.

The leading cities of Canaan, which include Hevron, Yarmot, Lachish, and Eglon, join forces to attack Givon for betraying their alliance against the Israelites. Now Givon is under a heavy attack by the Canaanites.

The men of Givon sent to Yehoshua at the camp in Gilgal, saying: "Do not slack your hands from your servants. Come to us quickly, and save us, and help us, for all the kings of the Amorites that dwell in the hill country are gathered together against us."

Yehoshua's covenant that he gave to the Givonites is so binding that he cannot go back on it and will not ignore their call for help.

So Yehoshua went up from Gilgal, he, and all the people of war with him, and all the mighty men of valor.

Yehoshua could have said, "It's none of my business. It's an inside matter between the Canaanites. Besides, the Givonites lied to me, so I owe them nothing. Let them kill each other." And he could have ignored their rescue call. But Yehoshua did not.

Yehoshua came upon them suddenly. He went up from Gilgal during the night. And the Lord disgraced them before Israel, and slew them with a great slaughter at Givon. They chased them by the way of the ascent of Beit Horon.

While Yehoshua is doing his part in the war, God is also doing His part.

The Lord cast down great stones from heaven...and they died. There were more who died with the hailstones, than whom the Children of Israel slew with the sword.

At this point, the battle day is about to end. The sun is about to set and the moon is about to rise. Because darkness is about to take over, the results of the entire military effort are about to waste away. Yehoshua desperately needs more time to finish the job.

So...

Yehoshua spoke to the Lord in the day when the Lord delivered up the Amorites before the Children of Israel. And he said in the sight of Israel: "Sun, stand still upon Givon; and Moon, in the Valley of Ayalon."

Yehoshua orders the sun and the moon to stand still for another ten hours until he finishes the war.

The sun stood still, and the moon stayed, until the nation had avenged themselves of their enemies.

This is something that never happened before and will never happen again, when the giants of creation, the sun and the moon, follow the orders of a human being.

There was no day like that before it or after it, that the Lord obeyed the voice of a man.

And the reason is...

The Lord fought for Israel.

The Talmud explains the reason that the sun and the moon stand still for Yehoshua is because he kept his word to the people of Givon. He made this enormous effort to come and help the Givonites because his covenant was bound by the name of the God of Israel. *(Beresheet Raba 6:9)*

Today, after 2,000 years of barrenness, cotton and grapes are growing again in the Valley of Ayalon, the valley that witnessed this incredible event.

As a result of Yehoshua's order, the schedule of the time of the world is delayed by ten hours. When and how the time will return to its original schedule is found in the story of Hezekayia, which happens 700 years later.

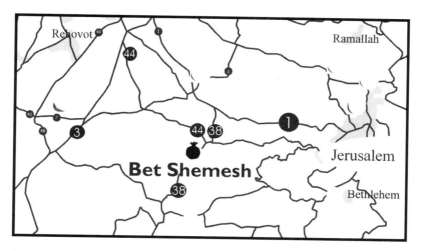

In The Time Of The Judges
Judges: 12, 13

Bet Shemesh

fter the death of Yehoshua, there is no strong leadership, so the spiritual influence from the surrounding Canaanite nations begins to affect the Israelite tribes.

The Children of Israel dwelled among the Canaanites, the Hittites, the Amorites, the Perizites, the Hivites, and the Jebusites. They took their daughters to be their wives, and gave their own daughters to their sons, and served their gods. The Children of Israel did evil in the sight of the Lord, and forgot the Lord their God, and served the Baalim and the Asherot.

Because the behavior of the Israelite nation is so unacceptable to God, He sends enemies against them. This is a time when each tribe has to protect itself and manage on its own without depending on their brother tribes for any help.

In the time of the Judges, the land on the southern coast of Israel is settled by the tribe of Dan, who is known as a strong tribe, symbolized by the snake. Their capital is the city of Bet Shemesh.

Dan is a tribe that understands the secrets of commerce. They manage to peacefully and successfully cultivate their portion, making the soil rich and fertile for their agriculture. Some of the men in this tribe make their living from the sea.

99

Southwest to the tribe of Dan, the Philistines have settled along the southern coast, but they are not good neighbors. Relations between Dan and the Philistines are hostile and the Philistines are Dan's most bitter enemy.

One of the most remarkable Judges during this time was Shimshon. For good reason, the Tanach begins the story of Shimshon's birth by first telling us...

The Children of Israel again did that which was evil in the sight of the Lord, and the Lord delivered them into the hand of the Philistines for 40 years.

Pressure from the Philistine enemy is growing stronger and more severe every day. The people of Dan ask God to help them against this southern enemy.

So the Tanach relates the story of the birth of Shimshon, who becomes the defender of the Israelites from the hands of the Philistines. Shimshon was born to a barren couple, who for many years prayed for a son.

At this time, there is a Judge in Israel, Evtzan, who is also known as Boaz, the same person from the story of Ruth.

The Tanach allots two verses to Boaz.

And after him Evtzan of Beit Lechem judged Israel. He had 30 sons, and 30 daughters he sent abroad, and 30 daughters he brought in from abroad for his sons. And he judged Israel seven years.

Boaz was an exceptionally powerful man. Having 60 boys and girls obviously meant that he had more than one wife. Each wife had a house for herself. And to have that many houses, surely large resources were needed.

The Talmud (*Bava Batra 91a*) adds another detail. When Boaz married off each of his sons and daughters, he gave two parties. One was in his house and the other was in the house of the in-laws. Boaz spent a lot of money on these weddings. He could afford it. And many people were invited to celebrate with Boaz the Judge, except for one man, Manoach.

The Talmud tells us that Boaz could not afford to invite Manoach, so the obvious question is how can that be? But another question that follows is why should he invite Manoach? We know that Boaz is from the tribe of Yehuda and Manoach is from Dan. So what is the connection?

The Talmud points out that Boaz should have invited Manoach because – they are related. Manoach is married to the niece of Boaz. But family relations were not enough. He still did not invite him.

The Talmud further explains, strangely, that Boaz did not invite Manoach, thinking that since he is a barren man who will not have children, he will never be able to reciprocate with an invitation back to his child's wedding. So 120 times, while many people are invited to the weddings of Boaz the Judge, Manoach is always left at home, humiliated.

And so the Talmud explains that because of this arrogance of Boaz, all of his sons and daughters died during his lifetime, one after the other. The man who is so powerful, so rich, becomes poor, old, and miserable. And when his last child is buried, all of a sudden, Manoach's wife gets pregnant. When their son is born, he is given the name Shimshon.

> The name Shimshon means, in Hebrew, *tov may sheesheem,* "better than 60."
>
> This name, given by Shimshon's mother, refers to the children of Boaz who died because of the haughtiness of their father – one living child is better than 60 dead children. *(Midrash Tanchuma 2)*

The woman bore a son, and called his name Shimshon. The child grew and the Lord blessed him.

And so, from the sin of arrogance, Boaz is punished by losing his wealth, honor, and family, while Shimshon, who is his mother's gift to God, becomes the shield of Israel.

Later, Shimshon becomes a Judge after Boaz and he defends Israel from the Philistines.

And the spirit of the Lord began to move him in Machaneh Dan, between Zorah and Eshtaol.

The Tanach presents a detailed account of the birth of Shimshon and describes how Shimshon's parents had to prepare for the birth of a very special son.

There was a certain man of Zorah, of the family of Dan, whose name was Manoach. And his wife was barren, and bore not.

The angel of the Lord appeared to the woman, and said to her: "You are barren now, and have not born, but you will conceive and bear a son. Therefore beware. Drink no wine or strong drink, and do not eat any unclean thing. You will conceive and bear a son. No razor will come upon his head, for the child will be a Nazirite to God from the womb. He will begin to save Israel out of the hand of the Philistines."

Then the woman came and told her husband, saying: "A man of God came to me, and his countenance was like the countenance of the angel of God, very terrible. I did not ask him where he came from and he did not tell me his name.

But he said to me: "You will conceive and bear a son. And now drink no wine or strong drink, and do not eat any unclean thing for the child will be a Nazirite to God from the womb to the day of his death."

Then Manoach appealed the Lord, and said: "Lord, let the man of God whom You sent, come again to us and teach us what we will do to the child that will be born."

God listened to the voice of Manoach. And the angel of God came again to the woman as she sat in the field, but Manoach her husband was not with her.

And the woman made haste and ran, and told her husband, and said to him: "The man appeared to me, who came to me that day."

And Manoach arose and went after his wife and came to

the man, saying to him: "Are you the man that spoke to the woman?" And he said: "I am."

And Manoach said: "Now when your word comes true, what will be the rule for the child, and what will be done with him?"

And the angel of the Lord said to Manoach: "Of all that I said to the woman, let her beware. She may not eat anything that comes from the grapevine. Nor drink wine or strong drink. Any unclean thing she shall not eat. All that I commanded her, let her observe."

Manoach said to the angel of the Lord: "Let us detain you, so that we may make ready a kid for you."

The angel of the Lord said to Manoach: "Though you detain me, I will not eat of your bread. And if you will make ready a burnt-offering, you must offer it to the Lord." For Manoach did not know that he was the angel of the Lord.

And Manoach said to the angel of the Lord: "What is your name, that when your words come to pass, we may do you honor?"

And the angel of the Lord said to him: "Why do you ask for my name, seeing it is hidden?"

So Manoach took the kid with the meal-offering, and offered it upon the rock to the Lord. The angel did wondrously and Manoach and his wife looked on. For it came to pass, when the flame went up toward heaven from off the altar, that the angel of the Lord ascended in the flame of the altar. And Manoach and his wife watched and they fell on their faces to the ground.

But the angel of the Lord did no more appear to Manoach or to his wife. Then Manoach knew that he was the angel of the Lord. Manoach said to his wife: "We will surely die, because we have seen God."

But his wife said to him: "If the Lord wanted to kill us, He would not have received a burnt-offering and a meal-offering at our hand, neither would He have shown us all these things, nor would He at this time have told such things as these."

In The Time Of The Judges
Judges: 15

Ein HaKoreh

oday, in the area of Ein HaKoreh, you will find the city of Rishon Lezion, which is where one of the Jewish pioneering ventures began in 1882. After many centuries of being barren and swampy, this land has been turned into a thriving modern Israeli city.

In order to get to the story of the source of the name Ein HaKoreh, we have to go back more than 3,000 years to the time of the Judges. This story is the last part of a chain of events between Shimshon and the Philistines.

Shimshon, who is the Judge of Israel, is behaving like a one-man army, constantly seeking confrontation with the Philistines, doing whatever he can to put them into embarrassing situations. To further annoy them, he goes to the Philistinian city, Timna, looking for one of their women to take for a wife.

Shimshon went down to Timna, and saw a woman in Timna of the daughters of the Philistines. He came up, and told his father and his mother, saying: "I have seen a woman in Timna of the daughters of the Philistines. Now take her for me as a wife."

Shimshon's need to constantly harass the Philistines continues even during the middle of his wedding celebration when he asks the Philistines a riddle they cannot answer.

Shimshon said to them: "Let me now put forth a riddle to you. If you can declare it to me within the seven days of the feast, and find it out, then I will give you thirty linen garments and thirty changes of raiment, but if you cannot declare it to me, then you will give me thirty linen garments and thirty changes of clothing." And they said to him: "Put forth the riddle, that we may hear it."

So now the way for the fight has been paved.

He said to them: "Out of the eater came forth food, and out of the strong came forth sweetness." And they could not in three days declare the riddle.

This riddle referred to Shimshon's killing of the lion that attacked him on his way to the wedding.

Then Shimshon went down, and his father and his mother, to Timna, and came to the vineyards of Timna. There a young lion roared against him. The spirit of the Lord came mightily upon him, and he tore him as one would have torn a kid, and he had nothing in his hand. But he did not tell his father or his mother what he had done.

After a while, he returned to take her (his wife). He turned aside to see the carcass of the lion. There was a swarm of bees in the body of the lion, and honey.

The Philistines could not figure out the riddle by themselves. In order not to let the Israelite outwit them, they turned to his new Philistine wife and threatened her to find out the answer.

"We will burn you and your father's house with fire. Have you called us to impoverish us?"

So Shimshon's wife starts nagging him for the answer.

Shimshon's wife wept before him, saying: "You hate me and do not love me. You have put forth a riddle to the children of my people, and you will not tell it to me?"

He said to her: "Behold, I have not told it to my father nor my mother, and will I tell you?"

Shimshon could not bear this pressure from his wife.

She wept before him the seven days, while their feast lasted. It came to pass on the seventh day, that he told her, because she pressed him sore.

She told the riddle to the children of her people.

When the time comes, with a big smile on their faces, the Philistines tell Shimshon the answer. Shimshon is furious for the dishonest way that they arrive at the answer. So he decides to act...

The spirit of the Lord came mightily upon him, and he went down to Ashkelon, and smote thirty of their men, and took their spoil, and gave the changes of clothes to those that declared the riddle.

And his anger was kindled, and he went up to his father's house.

Later on, the Philistines take Shimshon's wife and give her to the Philistine man that Shimshon challenged in the riddle. And when Shimshon comes to his wife, her father tells him that she has been given to the other man. At this point, Shimshon is outraged.

Shimshon said to them: "This time I will be blameless with the Philistines, when I do mischief to them."

Shimshon's revenge is to destroy the Philistine's grain crop.

Shimshon went and caught three hundred foxes, and took torches, and turned tail to tail, and put a torch in the midst between every two tails.

When he had set the torches on fire, he let them go into the standing corn of the Philistines, and burned up both the shocks and the standing corn, and also the olive yards.

According to the Talmud, Shimshon deliberately uses foxes to destroy the grain fields of the Philistines because a fox is an animal that can backstep. And that is exactly what the Philistines did to Shimshon – they backstepped on their decision to give him the woman from Timna. *(Sota p10)*

The destruction of a full year's crop provokes the Philistines to hunt Shimshon to kill him.

Then the Philistines went up, and camped in Yehuda, and spread themselves against Lehi. The men of Yehuda said: "Why did you come up against us?" And they said: "To bind Shimshon, we have come, to do to him as he has done to us."

The people of Yehuda now turn to Shimshon telling him "Your actions are causing problems for us with the Philistines and we want to turn you over to them."

Shimshon does not object to being turned over to the Philistines. His only concern is not to be in a confrontation with his brothers, so he asks them not to harm him.

They said to him: "We have come down to bind you, that we may deliver you into the hand of the Philistines." And Shimshon said to them: "Swear to me, that you will not fall upon me yourselves."

So Shimshon finds himself tied and barehanded in front of thousands of revengeful Philistines who want to kill him.

The Philistines shouted as they met him. The spirit of the Lord came mightily upon him. The ropes that were on his arms became as flax that was burned with fire and his bands dropped from off his hands.

Shimshon looks around to find some kind of weapon.

He found a jawbone of an ass, and put out his hand, and took it, and smote a thousand men with it.

Even Shimshon is surprised that he managed to kill a thousand men with the jawbone of a donkey. He forgets that it is God who is the real source of his might and mistakenly names the place of victory, *Ramat Lehi*, which means "after the jawbone."

Suddenly Shimshon becomes very thirsty and tired.

He was very thirsty, and called on the Lord, saying: "You have given this great deliverance by the hand of Your servant. Now will I die for thirst, and fall into the hand of the uncircumcised?"

It looks like Shimshon understands that he made a mistake in naming the area after the jawbone and himself, instead of attributing the victory to God. He turns to God and asks for forgiveness. God forgives Shimshon and provides him with water, straight from the jawbone.

But God cleaved the hollow place that is in Lehi, and there came water. When he had drunk, his spirit came back, and he revived.

According to the Talmud, Shimshon is too tired to reach the water coming from the jawbone, so God has mercy on him and directs the water straight from the jawbone to Shimshon's mouth. *(Beresheet Raba c98, s18)*

Shimshon is grateful to God for hearing him and saving him so he renames the place Ein HaKoreh, which means *"the spring of the caller."*

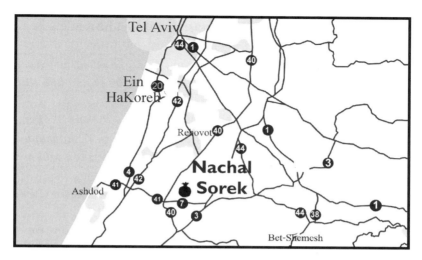

In The Time Of The Judges
Judges: 16

Nachal Sorek

N achal Sorek is a place today where the city of Yavneh has developed. Until today, it is an important valley that takes the floodwaters from Mount Scopus in Jerusalem and directs the waters all the way to the coast.

Along the valley, there was a Philistine city that was known as Sorek, where Delilah, the Philistine woman who attracted the heart of Shimshon lived.

The Philistine leaders who knew of Shimshon's weakness for Philistine women, said to her...

"Entice him, and see where his great strength rests, and by what means we may prevail against him, that we may bind him to afflict him. We will give you, from everyone of us, eleven hundred pieces of silver."

So that is exactly what she does.

Delilah said to Shimshon: "Tell me where your great strength lies, and where you might be bound to harm you."

And Shimshon said to her: "If they bind me with seven fresh bowstrings that were never dried, then will I become weak, and be as any other man."

Then the lords of the Philistines brought up to her seven fresh bowstrings which had not been dried, and she bound him with them.

Now she had an ambush unit waiting in the inner chamber. And she said to him: "The Philistines are upon you, Shimshon." He broke the bowstrings as a string of rope is broken when it touches the fire. So his strength was not known.

And Delilah said to Shimshon: "You have mocked me, and told me lies. Now tell me where you might be bound."

And he said to her: "If they only bind me with new ropes where no work has been done, then will I become weak, and be as any other man."

So Delilah took new ropes, and bound him, and said to him: "The Philistines are upon you, Shimshon." And the ambush unit waited in the inner chamber. And he broke them off his arms like a thread.

And Delilah said to Shimshon: "Until this time you have mocked me, and told me lies. Tell me where you should be bound."

And he said to her: "If you weave the seven locks of my head with the web."

And she fastened it with the pin, and said to him: "The Philistines are upon you, Shimshon." And he awoke out of his sleep, and plucked away the pin of the beam, and the web.

Feeling that she is about to lose 1,100 pieces of silver, Delilah turns to Shimshon, saying....

"How can you say 'I love you' when your heart is not with me? You have mocked me these three times, and have not told me where your great strength lies."

And when she pressed him daily with her words and urged him, that his soul was vexed to death.

Just as Shimshon was all-powerful against men, Delilah exposed his weakness to women... And so he opens his heart to her.

He told her all his heart, and said to her: "There has not come a razor upon my head, for I have been a Nazirite to God from my mother's womb. If I am shaven, then my strength will go from me, and I will become weak, and be like any other man."

As soon as Delilah sees that Shimshon is sincere and truthful with her, she calls the leader of the Philistines telling him "I have your enemy in my hands. Don't forget to bring the money."

When Delilah saw that he had told her all his heart, she sent and called for the lords of the Philistines, saying: "Come up this once, for he has told me all his heart." Then the lords of the Philistines came to her, and brought the money in their hand.

The rest of the job to earn the money is very easy for Delilah.

And she made him sleep upon her knees. She called for a man and had the seven locks of his head shaven off. She began to afflict him and his strength went from him.

And she said: "The Philistines are upon you, Shimshon." And he awoke out of his sleep, and said: "I will go out like the other times, and shake myself."

But he did not know that the Lord had departed from him.

The Philistines laid hold on him and put out his eyes. They brought him down to Gaza, and bound him with fetters of brass. He did grind in the prison.

Then the hair of his head began to grow again after he was shaven.

In The Time Of The Judges
Judges: 16

Shimshon in Gaza

The seaside city of Gaza was the home of the Philistine idol, Dagon. After Shimshon lost his power in Nachal Sorek when Delilah shaved his hair, he was brought to Gaza as a prisoner of the Philistines. He was held captive in Dagon's temple. This man, Shimshon, who once challenged the entire army of the Philistines and beat them, is now humiliated and being lead powerless to his cruel death.

Dagon's temple is a huge building that can hold thousands of people. On that day, everybody wanted to join the big festival of killing the greatest enemy of the Philistines.

And the lords of the Philistines gathered them together to offer a great sacrifice to Dagon their god, and to rejoice, saying: "Our god has delivered Shimshon our enemy into our hand."

And when the people saw him, they praised their god saying: "Our god has delivered into our hand our enemy, and the destroyer of our country, who has slain many of us."

And so the Philistines are ready to begin their festival.

After their hearts were merry, they said: "Call for Shimshon, that he may make us sport." And they called for Shimshon from the prison and he made sport before them. They set him between the pillars.

Something very unexpected happens when the Jewish prisoner is placed between the two pillars. The prisoner seems

to lean on the pillars, which support the structure of the building. He manages to move them so that the entire temple collapses, killing all the Philistines inside and on the roof.

*Now the house was full of men and women. All the lords of
the Philistines were there. And there were on the roof about three
thousand men and women that beheld while Shimshon made sport.*

One prayer allows Shimshon to get back his power.

*Shimshon called to the Lord, and said: "Lord God, remem-
ber me, and strengthen me, only this once, God, that I may be this
once avenged of the Philistines for my two eyes."*

*And Shimshon took grasp of the two middle pillars upon
which the house rested, and leaned upon them, the one with his
right hand, and the other with his left.*

And Shimshon said: "Let me die with the Philistines."

*And he bent with all his might and the house fell upon the
lords and upon all the people that were therein. So the dead that
he slew at his death were more than he slew all his life.*

Shimshon, the
boy who was born after
many years to a barren
couple, Manoach and
Slalphonet, who came to
be the Judge of Israel
and saved Israel from
the hands of the Philis-
tines, dies under these
circumstances.

The Talmud explains that God has
treated Shimshon measure for
measure.

Shimshon, who misuses his eyes
to chase Philistine women, loses his
sight when he is blinded by the very
same Philistines. *(Sota, p9)*

*Then his brethren and all the house of his father came
down, and took him, and brought him up, and buried him between
Zorah and Eshtaol in the burial plot of Manoach his father. And
he judged Israel twenty years.*

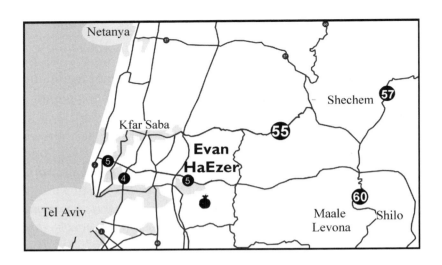

In The Time Of The Judges
Shmuel 1: 4

Evan HaEzer

Near the end of the time of the Judges and before the time of the Kings, the Philistines take advantage of a couple of events which allows them to sneak into the territory of the Israelites and take control of more land.

Now that Shimshon, the great Judge and defender of Israel against the Philistines is dead, the people of Dan are afraid of the Philistinian revenge. So they abandon their land and flee from the Philistines to the northern part of Israel.

There is no king in Israel, as mentioned many times in the Tanach, to unite the tribes against the Philistinian threat.

While the original location of the Philistines was on the southern coast near Gaza and Ashkelon, we find now the battlefield between the Philistines and Israel takes place in Evan HaEzer, in the central part of Israel, very close to Shilo, which was the capital of Israel at that time.

Now Israel went out against the Philistines to battle and camped beside Evan HaEzer. The Philistines camped in Afek.

The battle is tough.

The Israelites have casualties....

And the Philistines put themselves in a pack against Israel. When the battle spread, Israel was smitten before the Philistines. They slew the army in the field, about four thousand men.

The people of Israel are puzzled...

And when the people came into the camp, the elders of Israel said: "Why has the Lord smitten us today before the Philistines? Let us get the Ark of the Covenant of the Lord from Shilo so that He may come among us, and save us out of the hand of our enemies."

It looks like an easy solution has been found. The Ark of the Covenant will be brought to the battlefield. That, for sure, is going to help save Israel from the hands of the Philistines ...they think.

So the people went to Shilo. They brought from there the Ark of the Covenant of the Lord of Hosts, who sits upon the Cherubim. And the two sons of Eli, Hophni and Pinchas, were there with the Ark of the Covenant of God.

So the Ark of the Covenant is brought from Shilo to the battlefield. Eli, the Kohen, does not agree with this idea, but he is too old to argue about it. With a lot of fears, he lets the Ark of the Covenant be taken to the battlefield.

When the Ark of the Covenant of the Lord came into the camp, all Israel shouted with a great shout, so that the earth rang.

The arrival of the Ark of the Covenant is so exciting that even the Philistines, in their camp, can sense it.

When the Philistines heard the noise of the shout, they said: "What means the noise of this great shout in the camp of the Hebrews?" And they knew that the Ark of the Lord had come into the camp.

The next morning, in the course of the battle, it looks like the Ark of the Covenant does not help. Israel is defeated. There is a

> Who is the Philistine soldier that takes the Ark of the Covenant? ...Goliath!
> *(Midrash Shmuel 2: 11;1)*

> Who is the Philistine soldier that kills Hophni and Pinchas while they are carrying the Ark? ...Goliath!
> *(Midrash Shmuel 2: 11;1)*

massive slaughter. About 30,000 men are killed and many others flee for their lives. And the Ark of the Covenant falls into the hands of the Philistines.

The Philistines fought, and Israel was smitten, and they fled, every man to his tent. There was a very great slaughter. For there fell of Israel, thirty thousand men. And the Ark of God was taken and the two sons of Eli, Hophni and Pinchas, were slain.

There is one soldier who manages to run back to Shilo to tell Israel and Eli the Kohen all that happened in the battle.

> We learn from the Talmud that the soldier who reports back to Eli is Shaul, the man who later becomes the first king of Israel.
> *(Midrash Shmuel 2: 11;1)*

And there ran a man of Benjamin out of the army and he came to Shilo the same day with his clothes rent and with earth upon his head.

So here is Israel's mistake. They depend on the idea that the Ark of the Covenant will save them from their enemy, instead of depending on God. Not only are they not saved, but a terrible catastrophe has happened with the holy Ark of the Covenant.

The Midrash *(Beresheet Raba 54)* has a special perspective on this event at Evan HaEzer as it was something that God had already told Avraham. The Midrash takes us back to the time of Avraham and Avimelech, the king of the Philistines.

Knowing that Avraham is going to own the land, Avimelech comes to him and asks for a covenant not to send away his descendants. Avraham agrees and brings seven lambs for the covenant, which leads to this place being known as Be'er Sheva.

God turns to Avraham and says, "How can you share a present that I gave you, the land of Israel, with My enemy, the Philistines. And so, listen to what is going to happen.

"Because you gave him seven lambs, seven kings from his descendants will rule the country before the first king of Israel.

"Seven temples of your descendants will be destroyed by his descendants.

"Seven righteous men are going to be killed by his descendants .

"And, the Ark of the Covenant will be taken by his descendants and held captive for seven months."

Today, on the very land where this battle took place more than 3,000 years ago, is the Jewish city of Rosh Ha'Ayan.

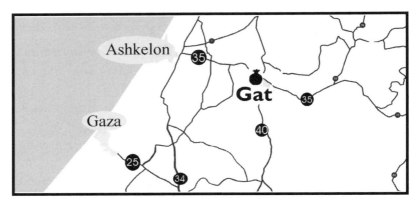

In The Time Of Shaul
Shmuel 1: 21

Gat

After David kills Goliath, King Shaul becomes deadly jealous and treats David as a threat to his crown.

David sees enough signs to indicate that Shaul is determined to kill him, as the king declares in the presence of his son, Yonaton.

"For as long as the son of Yishai lives on the earth, you will not be established, nor your kingdom. Therefore, send now and bring him to me, for he deserves to die."

Although David did no wrong to the king, Shaul still wants to kill him. And so David flees to find shelter with the Philistines. He runs to their city of Gat.

David arose and fled that day for fear of Shaul and went to Achish, the king of Gat.

Gat is the city of Goliath. It is fresh in everyone's mind that Goliath died at hand of David. So you would think that David would do everything he could to get as far away as possible from this place. But that is not David's strategy.

David decides to go to the very place where nobody would think to look for him. David is hoping to mingle among the people and disappear.

However...

The servants of Achish said to him: "Is not this David the king of the land? Did they not sing one to another of him in dances, saying: Shaul has slain his thousands, and David his ten thousands?"

Not only has David been exposed, but his role in the victories of Israel over the Philistines has been vocally mentioned to King Achish.

David is apprehensive now.

And David laid up these words in his heart, and was very afraid of Achish, the king of Gat.

On the very day that David went to the Philistines in Gat, God turned to David and said, "To Gat you are going? Yesterday you killed Goliath.

The Midrash tells us of a previous conversation between David and God.

David turns to God and says, "Everything You did in Your world is wonderful, except for one thing, foolishness. What is good about a fool walking in a market, tearing up his clothes and the people laughing and the kids running after him? Does it look good in Your eyes?"

And God answers David, "Foolishness, you think is unnecessary? Be sure that you are going to need it! And you will pray to Me and ask for it." *(Yalcut Shimoni, Shmuel I, c247)*

His blood is still fresh. Not only are you going to Gat, but the sword of Goliath is in your hand and his brothers are the bodyguards of the king."

When word spread that David is in the city, he is found and brought to the king.

Goliath's brothers turn to the king and say, "Let us kill who killed our brother." The king answers, "It was a war. He killed him in a war. And if Goliath had killed David, then what?"

So the brothers of Goliath said, "If it was a war, then what about the terms of the war. Goliath claimed whoever is defeated will be the slave of the other. So you must give your throne to David."

"If he is able to fight with me and kill me, then we will be your servants. But if I prevail against him, and kill him, then you will be our servants, and serve us."
(Shmuel 1: 17)

At this point, David becomes very afraid and turns to God and says, "Please God, help me become an absolute fool so that the king of Gat will not see me as a threat to his crown and will leave me alone."

And God hears David.

David starts to behave like a fool, screaming and writing ridiculous claims on the gates of Gat that the king of Gat owes him 100,000 pieces of silver while the wife of the king owes him 50,000 pieces of silver. At the same time, the daughter of Achish, who really was a fool, was screaming inside the house while David was screaming wildly outside. You can imagine the pandemonium.

The Tanach says...

He changed his demeanor before them and feigned himself mad in their hands. He scribbled on the doors of the gate, and let his spittle fall down upon his beard.

David was so impressive in his role as the fool that Achish, who was watching this crazy situation, turned to his servants...

"When you see a man that is mad, why do you bring him to me? Do I lack madmen. You brought this fellow to play the madman in my presence? Shall this fellow come into my house?"

And so Gat is the place where David will remember that he had to use a very special trick, that of being a fool, in order to survive and outwit his enemies.

From this event in Gat, David composed Psalm 34.

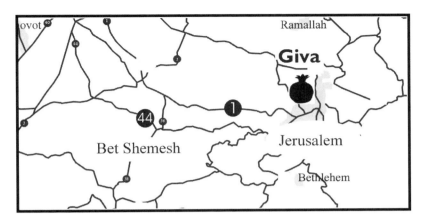

In The Time Of The Judges
Judges: 19, 20, 21

Giva

In the Jerusalem neighborhood of Pisgat Ze'ev, there is an unfinished structure on a high hill that was started in 1965 by King Hussein of Jordan. The king did not realize that he was constructing his palace on the exact location of the ruins of King Shaul's palace, which preserves the name *Givat Shaul*, the hill of Shaul.

The Jordanian king, who at that time ruled this area of Yehuda and Shomron, wanted to have a summer palace on one of the highest mountains in the land of Benjamin, which used to be called Tel El Ful, by the neighboring Arabs.

Pisgat Ze'ev is located on the outskirts of the ruins of Giva between Jerusalem in the south and Rama in the north. This biblical city was located on the Road Of The Patriarchs, which has been called by this name for centuries because the Patriarchs, Avraham, Yitzhok, and Yaakov traveled on this very road on their journeys throughout the Land of Israel.

Our story deals with a horrible incident which happened in the time of the Judges in Giva. This incident links us to other very important stories in Tanach.

A man, with his concubine, arrives at the gate of the city before darkness, looking for a place to stay the night.

When they were by Yevus, it was late in the day and the

servant said to his master, "Come, and let us turn into this city of the Yevus, and lodge here."

And his master said to him, "We will not turn into the city of a foreigner that is not of the Children of Israel, but we will pass over to Giva."

And he said to his servant, "Come and let us continue to one of these places and we will lodge in Giva, or in Rama."

So they continued and went their way. The sun set on them near Giva, which belonged to Benjamin.

The man is on his way to his house in Maale Levona, which is in the land of Efraim, another day's walk north. He is coming from Beit Lechem, were he took his concubine from her father's house.

Now the man is waiting to be invited to stay in one of the houses, but it seems like no one is showing any interest in offering hospitality to the strangers.

They turned to go to lodge in Giva. He went in and sat down in the city square. There was no man that took them into his house to lodge.

Finally, an old man, returning from the fields, asks him, "Where are you going to stay the night and why are you waiting at the gate?"

There came an old man from his work out of the field that evening. Now the man was from the hill country of Efraim and he sojourned in Giva, but the men of the place were Benjamites.

The old man invites the couple to stay with him and even invites them to wash and to eat. In the middle of the meal, evil people from the city come to the house demanding to take the guests in order to molest them. The old man tries to convince the Benjamites not to do this evil thing, but they insist and take the woman.

The men would not listen to him. So the man laid hold on his concubine and brought her to them, and they knew her and abused her all night until morning. When the day began to spring, they let her go.

Then the woman came back in the dawning of the day and fell at the door of the man's house where her man was.

In the morning...

Her man rose up and opened the doors of the house, and was on his way. Behold, the woman, his concubine, had fallen at the door of the house, with her hands upon the threshold.

The man realizes she is dead when...

He said to her, "Get up, and let us go." But there was no answer.

And so...

He took her up on the ass. And the man rose up, and they went to his house.

Then...

He took a knife and laid hold on his concubine, and divided her, limb by limb, into twelve pieces, and sent her throughout all the borders of Israel.

The tribes of Israel are shocked...

"Such a thing has not happened nor been seen from the day that the Children of Israel came up out of the land of Egypt until this day."

In those days, justice and law were not practiced. The people of Israel faced a horrible moral deterioration and this story is just one example.

For a very good reason, it is clear why this chapter starts and ends with a remark that...

In those days, when there was no king in Israel ... every man did that which was right in his own eyes.

The story of what happened in Giva shocks the people like an earthquake. The people of Israel gather at Mizpah to consult and decide how to react.

Then all the Children of Israel went out and the congregation was unified as one man, from Dan even to Be'er Sheva, with the land of Gilad, to the Lord at Mizpah.

And they conclude...

"We will not leave, any of us, to go to his tent, nor will any of us return to his house...

...until justice will be done and the evil people will pay for what they did.

Now deliver the men, the base fellows that are in Giva, that we may put them to death, and put away evil from Israel."

It looks like the people of Benjamin are not going to respond.

But the Children of Benjamin would not listen to the voice of their brothers, the Children of Israel.

The Tanach, at this point, describes the fighting skills of the men of Benjamin.

And the Children of Benjamin numbered on that day, out of the cities, twenty-six thousand men that drew sword, besides the inhabitants of Giva, who numbered seven hundred chosen men.

All these people, even seven hundred chosen men, were left-handed. Every one could sling stones at a hairbreadth, and not miss.

Facing them were...

The men of Israel, beside Benjamin, who numbered four hundred thousand men that drew sword. All these were men of war.

By the end of the battle day between the people of Israel and the men of Benjamin...

The Children of Benjamin came forth out of Giva, and destroyed down to the ground of the Israelites, on that day twenty and two thousand men.

The day after does not look any better for the other tribes.

The Children of Israel came near against the Children of Benjamin the second day. And Benjamin went forth against them out of Giva the second day, and destroyed down to the ground of the Children of Israel again, eighteen thousand men. All these drew the sword.

Prior to the battle on the third day, the tribes of Israel...

...went up, and came to Beit El, and wept, and sat there

before the Lord. They fasted that day until the evening. And they offered burnt-offerings and peace-offerings before the Lord. The Children of Israel asked of the Lord – for the Ark of the Covenant of God was there in those days.

Pinchas, the son of Eleazar, the son of Aharon, stood before it in those days – saying: "Shall I yet again go out to battle against the Children of Benjamin my brother, or shall I stop?" And the Lord said: "Go up for tomorrow I will deliver him into your hand."

This time Israel is very anxious not only to win the battle with the people of Benjamin, but to wipe out the whole tribe...

So all who fell that day from Benjamin were twenty and five thousand men that drew the sword. All these were men of valor. But six hundred men turned and fled toward the wilderness to the rock of Rimmon, and dwelled at the rock of Rimmon for four months.

The men of Israel turned back upon the Children of Benjamin and smote them with the edge of the sword, both the entire city, and the cattle, and all that they found. Moreover, all the cities which they found, they set on fire.

And if that was not enough...

...the men of Israel had sworn in Mizpah, saying: "No one will give his daughter to Benjamin as a wife."

The vow that the tribes of Israel took to join in battle against Benjamin was so binding that when the tribes noticed that the people of Yavesh-Gilad did not send soldiers to join Israel...

The congregation sent twelve thousand of the most valiant men, and commanded them, saying: "Go and smite the inhabitants of Yavesh-Gilad with the edge of the sword, including the women and the boys."

And what about the girls?

And they found among the inhabitants of Yavesh-Gilad four hundred virgin girls who had not known a man and they brought them to the camp in Shilo, which is in the land of Canaan.

A while after, a new atmosphere replaced the anger and frustration towards Benjamin...

The whole congregation sent and spoke to the Children of Benjamin that were at the rock of Rimmon, and proclaimed peace with them.

The 400 girls of Yavesh-Gilad are given to 400 of the surviving men of Benjamin.

But what about the other 200 men?

Then the elders of the congregation said: "What can we do to provide wives for those who remain, for the women of Benjamin have been destroyed?"

So a very original solution was found.

They said: "There is the holiday of the Lord from year to year in Shilo, which is north of Beit El, on the east side of the highway that goes up from Beit El to Shechem, and south of Levona."

They commanded the Children of Benjamin, saying: "Go and lie in wait in the vineyards and see if the daughters of Shilo come out to dance in the dances. Then you come out of the vineyards and catch you, every man, his wife from the daughters of Shilo, and go to the land of Benjamin.

From this event, a new Jewish holiday has been established – *Tu B'Av*, the 15th day of the month of Av. This day is known as the day of the beginning of the grape harvest in the vineyards.

Ever since, this day is known to be one of the happiest days in the Jewish calendar, first because of the approval of accepting back the people of Benjamin to the congregation of Israel after almost being wiped out and second, because the grape harvest started on this day. All the girls of Israel would go down to the vineyards to celebrate in this beautiful event.

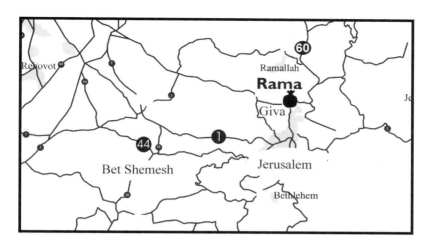

In The Time Of Shaul
Shmuel I: 8, 9, 10, 19

Rama

Rama is a city that was located on the Road Of The Patriarchs. Today the ruins of this city are settled by an Arab village El Ram, which preserves the name Rama.

Rama is mentioned for the first time in the Tanach in Shmuel 1, in the story of the birth of Shmuel. The next time the city is mentioned is in a story about a young man who is going on a journey to look for his father's lost donkeys.

The young man is Shaul ben Kish. After searching the area for three days, Shaul is about to give up when the boy that is with him, says...

"Behold now, there is in this city a man of God, and he is a man that is held in honor. All that he says comes to pass. Let us go there. Perhaps he can tell us, concerning our journey, where we go."

Shaul, who is concerned about how to meet the Prophet without anything to give him, does not know that the Prophet is actually waiting for him.

Now the Lord had revealed to Shmuel a day before Shaul came, saying: "Tomorrow about this time, I will send a man from the land of Benjamin, and you shall anoint him to be a ruler over

My people Israel."

Eventually Shaul decides to go and seek the Prophet Shmuel. As he walks up to the city, he sees girls walking down to the city well and asks them where the Prophet's house is.

The girls answer...

"He is, behold, he is before you. Hurry because he will come today to the city for the people have a sacrifice today in the high place. As soon as you are in the city, you shall quickly find him, before he goes to the high place to eat, for the people will not eat until he comes, because he will bless the sacrifice. Afterwards, they will eat from the sacrifice."

From the girls' answer, Shaul understands that an important ceremony is about to take place. So he rushes to the place where the people are gathering. As they pass through the gate to the city, Shaul turns to the man at the gate and asks...

"Tell me, where is the Prophet's house?"

Shaul doesn't know that he is actually speaking with the Prophet, who came down to meet him.

And Shmuel answered Shaul, and said: "I am the Prophet. Go up before me to the high place, for you shall eat with me today. In the morning, I will let you go, and will tell you all that is in your heart.

Regarding the lost donkeys...

And as for your donkeys that were lost three days ago, ease your mind for they have been found. Besides, to whom does all the desirable property belong, if not to you and your father's family.

The overwhelming respectable words of the Prophet put Shaul in shock, but he still has no idea of what is awaiting him.

And Shaul answered and said: "Am I not a Benjamite, of the smallest of the tribes of Israel? And my family the least of all the families of the tribe of Benjamin? Why do you speak to me in this way?"

So Shmuel takes Shaul and leads him forward...

And Shmuel took Shaul and his servant, and brought them

into the chamber, and made them sit in the best place among the people, who were about thirty persons.

Shmuel said to the cook: "Bring the portion which I gave you, of which I said to you: 'Set it by you.'"

The cook took up the thigh, and that which was on it, and set it before Shaul.

And Shmuel said: "Behold that which has been reserved! Set it before you and eat because the appointed time has been kept for you, for I said: 'I have invited the people.'"

So Shaul did eat with Shmuel that day.

Little by little, Shaul begins to understand that something very important is happening to him. After the people leave at the end of the meal, Shmuel invites Shaul to the roof and there he learns with Shmuel the laws of the Kingship of Israel.

When they came down from the high place into the city, he spoke with Shaul on the rooftop.

After studying all night...

Shmuel took the vial of oil, and poured it on Shaul's head, and kissed him, and said: "Is it not the Lord that has anointed you to be a ruler over His people?"

Shaul, who began this journey looking for lost donkeys, actually finds himself becoming the king of Israel.

Then all the elders of Israel gathered themselves together, and came to Shmuel in Rama. They said to him: "Behold, you are old, and your sons do not walk in your ways. Now make us a king to judge us like all the nations."

The tribes' demand to have a king, like all the other nations, has been answered in Rama, but the rule of Shaul over Israel lasts two years – two years only.

Two years later, the Tanach takes us back to Rama when Shaul's reign begins to fade.

After David heroically defeats Goliath in the battle at Emek Ha'Elah and saves Israel, he becomes an officer in the army of Shaul. He is given Shaul's daughter as his wife and is invited to live close to the king in his city, Giva. But the competition between the personalities of Shaul and David is too strong. Shaul cannot bear to hear and see the popularity of David reaching new heights every day. Ultimately, Shaul decides that David must be killed.

Shaul sent messengers to David's house, to watch him and to slay him in the morning.

Michal, David's wife, turns to David, saying...

"If you do not save your life tonight, then tomorrow you shall be slain."

David does not need any further explanation and so with his wife's help, he escapes through the window.

Michal let David down through the window. He went and fled and escaped.

Shaul is very anxious to see David dead, even if it means bringing him sick in his bed to the king.

Shaul sent the messengers to see David, saying: "Bring him up to me in the bed, that I may slay him."

When David's bed arrives...

There was a mannequin in the bed, with a quilt of goats' hair at its head.

Shaul realizes that he has been duped by David and his daughter. He is outraged. He turns to his daughter...

"Why have you deceived me like this and let my enemy escape?"

Despite the fact that she gave David full support, out of love to him, she lies...

"He said to me: Let me go. Why should I kill you?"

At this point, Shaul is no longer hiding his intention to kill David. He sends his intelligence people to look for him.

David escapes from Giva, and goes to the Prophet Shmuel in Rama, which is a short walk north of Giva. Very upset, David enters Shmuel's house, complaining that Shaul treats him very badly and even wants to kill him.

Now David fled and escaped and came to Shmuel to Rama and told him all that Shaul had done to him.

It seems like Shmuel is not really concerned with Shaul's behavior. Instead, he leads David to the roof of his house.

He and Shmuel went and stayed in Naiot.

Meanwhile, the intelligence information that is presented to Shaul is that David went to Rama and he is sitting with Shmuel on the roof.

It was told to Shaul, "Behold, David is at Naiot in Rama."

Shaul understands that David is sitting in the very place that he, Shaul, was sitting two years ago with Shmuel before being anointed to be the king of Israel. This information makes Shaul furious. Jealousy takes control of his personality. Shaul orders his soldiers to go to Rama to arrest David, in the house of Shmuel, and to bring him to Shaul to be killed.

> The Talmud clarifies the term *Naiot* as the issue that Shmuel and David were discussing. Naiot is the beauty of the world, which is the *Beit HaMikdash,* the Temple. It is here that Shmuel begins discussing with David the need to build the House of God. David and Shmuel get into a very deep spiritual discussion dealing with the details of how to construct the Beit HaMikdash. It was on this same rooftop, two years earlier, that Shmuel was teaching the laws of kingship to Shaul. *(Zevachim 54)*

Shaul sent messengers to take David.

As the soldiers of Shaul enter in the gates of Rama, the spirit of God inspires them. They become prophets.

The spirit of God came upon the messengers of Shaul, and they also prophesied...

"David is going to be the king of Israel."

Shaul hears what happened to his soldiers, so he sends another unit.

And when it was told to Shaul, he sent more messengers.

The same thing happens to the second unit. As they entered the gates of Rama, they prophesied, "David is going to be the king of Israel." At this point, David is aware that Shaul has sent soldiers to arrest him, to kill him. The first time, a miracle happens. The soldiers become prophets. The second time, again a miracle happens. The soldiers become prophets.

A regular person would think to himself that a miracle can happen once, maybe twice, but no more, so you had better save your life and run away. But not David. Studying with Shmuel the laws of building the Beit HaMikdash is much more important than anything else. David ignores the commotion surrounding him and stays with Shmuel.

But Shaul does not give up.

Shaul sent messengers again the third time, and they also prophesied.

When the third unit become prophets...

Shaul went to Rama...

Ahead of his army...

He asked and said: "Where is Shmuel and David?" And someone said: "Behold, they are at Naiot in Rama."

As he enters the gates of Rama...

The spirit of God came upon him also, and he went on, and prophesied, until he came to Naiot in Rama,

...saying, "David is going to be king of Israel."

And he also stripped off his clothes.

...the royal clothing.

He also prophesied before Shmuel.

For how much time did he prophesy?

All that day and all that night.

Even with this extraordinary experience that Shaul has, jealousy and hatred continue to drive him to chase David to kill him, though when cool-minded, Shaul knows that he is doing wrong to an innocent man.

Shaul will remember Shmuel's rooftop as the place where he was prepared to be the first king of Israel. David will remember the rooftop for the wonderful time he spent with Shmuel discussing the secret wonders of building the Beit HaMikdash.

The story of Shaul's chase after David and the people who cooperate with him continues in the city of Nov.

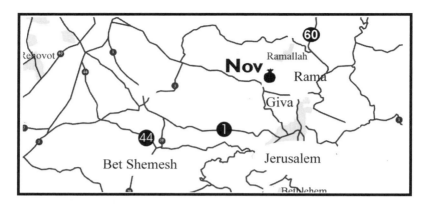

In The Time Of Shaul

Nov

Shmuel 1: 21, 22

A rocky hill located half a mile away from the end of the running field of the Atarot Airport of Jerusalem is considered by archeologists to be the city of Nov. Among the rocks you can find remains of thriving Jewish life from the first and second Temple periods like cisterns, wine pressing systems, and other artifacts. In that time the whole area was densely settled and cultivated.

The picture of the rocky hills of today reflects the neglect of the last 2,000 years, the hill country of Benjamin, as well as the rest of the country that turned into desert.

The Tanach takes us to this very hill, while it describes the way David becomes a homeless refugee.

After the experience David has in the house of Shmuel in Rama, when Shaul sent the army to arrest and kill him, it becomes clear to David and to everyone around, that King Shaul wants to kill him. He knows that he cannot expect help from anyone, including his tribe, Yehuda, or his family, because Shaul will consider them to be traitors.

David must develop a plan that will allow him to find shelter and basic needs somewhere. He feels lonely and forgotten. So David to turns to God and sings a wonderful song which we know as Chapter 23 in Psalms.

A Psalm of David. The Lord is my shepherd. I shall not want. He makes me to lie down in green pastures. He leads me beside the still waters. He restores my soul. He guides me in straight paths for His name's sake. Though I walk through the valley of the shadow of death, I will fear no evil, for You are with me. Your rod and Your staff, they comfort me. You prepare a table before me in the presence of my enemies. You have anointed my head with oil. My cup runs over. Surely goodness and mercy shall follow me all the days of my life and I shall dwell in the house of the Lord forever.

When David leaves the house of Shmuel in Rama, he goes to the city of Nov, a city inhabited only by Kohanim, which is where the Mishkan is located. David hopes that their position as Kohanim will shield them from Shaul's rage.

David turns to Achimelech, the Kohen Gadol and asks for some food.

"Now therefore what is under your hand? Five loaves of bread? Give them in my hand, or whatsoever there is present."

...and something to protect himself.

David said to Achimelech: "And is there perhaps here under your hand, a spear or sword?"

The excuse for these specific demands is that...

"The king has sent me on a mission and has said to me: 'Let no one know anything about this mission that I send you.'"

It was so urgent...

"I have neither brought my sword nor my weapons with me, because the king's mission required haste."

When Achimelech offers David the sword of Goliath...

"The sword of Goliath the Philistine, whom you slew in the valley of Elah, here it is wrapped in a cloth behind the ephod. If you will take that, take it for there is no other here, except for this."

David happily responds...

"There is none like that. Give it to me."

From here, David flees the borders of Israel and goes to Gat, Goliath's home, thinking that Gat is the last place anyone will look for him. "Here I can disappear."

Meanwhile, Shaul wakes up from the very special prophetic experience he had when he chased David to Rama.

The first question Shaul asks is "Where is David?"

The answer of his intelligence officer is, "We don't know."

Shaul feels like people are not telling him everything they know and that some information is being hidden from him. Bitterly, he turns to his officers saying...

"Hear now, you Benjamites. The son of Yeshai will give everyone of you fields and vineyards. He will make you all captains of thousands and captains of hundreds.

"You are all traitors!

"All of you have conspired against me, and there was none that disclosed it to me when my son made a pact with the son of Yeshai. None of you are sorry for me, or tells me that my son has stirred up my servant against me, to lie in wait, like today."

Shaul feels like the whole world is against him. This is probably one of the hardest moments in his life as the king.

At this point, one of Shaul's officers, Doeg HaEdomi, turns to the king saying...

"I saw the son of Yeshai coming to Nov, to Achimelech, the son of Achituv. He inquired of the Lord for him and gave him food and gave him the sword of Goliath the Philistine."

Shaul acts like a wounded animal.

Then the king sent for Achimelech the Kohen, the son of Achituv, and all his father's house, the Kohanim that were in Nov. They all came to the king.

The king, sharp as a knife, turns to the Kohen Gadol, Achimelech...

"Hear now, you son of Achituv."

And he answered: "Here I am, my lord."

And Shaul said to him: "Why have you conspired against me, you and the son of Yeshai, in that you have given him bread, and a sword, and have inquired of God for him, that he should rise against me, to lie in wait, like today."

Shaul's rage blinds him to see the innocent Kohanim standing before him.

Then Achimelech answered the king, and said: "And who among all your servants is so trusted as David, who is the king's son-in-law, and gives heed to your bidding, and is honorable in your house?"

Besides...

"Have I today begun to inquire of God for him? Be it far from me."

So please...

"Do not let the king impute anything to his servant, nor to all the house of my father for your servant knows nothing of all this, small or big."

But the king's spiritual condition prevents him from listening to anything.

And the king said: "You shall surely die, Achimelech, you, and all your father's house."

Then the king said to the guard that stood next to him: "Turn, and slay the Kohanim of the Lord."

But Shaul's servants simply cannot do it.

The servants of the king would not put forth their hand to fall upon the Kohanim of the Lord.

They just cannot do this horrible thing, to kill the innocent Kohanim, who obviously knew nothing and meant no harm to the king.

And so the king turned to the man who hated David the most, Doeg, saying...

"Turn you and fall upon the Kohanim."

And Doeg the Edomite turned and he fell upon the Kohanim, and he slew on that day eighty-five people that did wear a linen ephod.

The killing party continued...

And Nov, the city of the Kohanim, he killed with the edge of the sword, both men and women.

He did not have mercy on...

...the children and babies.

Nor did he exclude killing...

...oxen and asses and sheep, with the edge of the sword.

In the Talmud (*Yoma p22*), this event is compared to another event Shaul is involved with – the battle between Israel and Amalek.

The Talmud says that when Shaul had mercy on the king of Amalek, Agog, and the animals and did not kill them, a Voice came from heaven saying, "No need to be so righteous."

And here where obviously, Shaul was killing innocent people, an overkill which included men, women, children, and livestock, again a Voice came from heaven saying, "No need to be so evil."

The Talmud takes these stories and teaches a lesson for life.

Whenever you are too merciful to cruel people, the way Shaul was to Amalek, you will find yourself too cruel to merciful people, the way Shaul was to the people of Nov. *(Yoma 22)*

Only one man from the city of Nov and the family of Achimelech manage to escape the slaughter.

One of the sons of Achimelech, the son of Achituv, named Evyatar, escaped, and fled after David.

Evyatar runs away and joins David who promises him...

"*Sit with me. Do not be afraid. For he that seeks my life, seeks your life. For with me you shall be safe.*"

At this point Evyatar becomes David's ally.

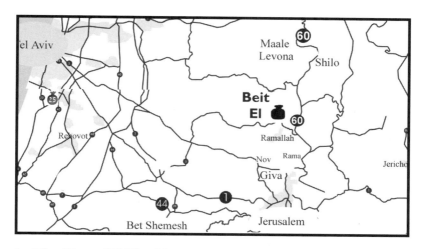

In The Time Of The Kings

Beresheet: 28, 35 ~ Kings 1: 11, 12, 13

Beit El

One of the most important cities on the Road Of The Patriarchs is Beit El, a city which sometimes belonged to the tribe of Benjamin and sometimes to the powerful neighboring tribe to the north, Efraim.

The first time Beit El is mentioned in the Tanach is in the story of Yaakov, fleeing the land after he took his father's blessing from his brother Esav.

And Yaakov went out from Be'er Sheva, and went toward Haran. He lighted upon the place and tarried there all night because the sun had set. He took one of the stones of the place and put it under his head and lay down in that place to sleep.

He dreamed and behold a ladder set up on the earth. The top of it reached to heaven. And behold the angels of God were ascending and descending on it.

The Lord stood beside him and said: "I am the Lord, the God of Avraham your father, and the God of Yitzhok. The land where you lay, to you will I give it, and to your descendants. Your descendants shall be as the dust of the earth and you shall spread abroad to the west, and to the east, and to the north, and to the south. And in you and in your descendants shall all the families of the earth be blessed. And, behold, I am with you and will keep you wherever you go, and will bring you back into this land. I will not leave you until I have done that which I have spoken to you."

Yaakov awoke from his sleep, and he said: "Surely the Lord is in this place and I did not know it." He was afraid, and said: "How awesome is this place! This is none other than the House of God, and this is the gate of heaven."

Yaakov rose up early in the morning and took the stone that he had put under his head and set it up for a pillar and poured oil upon the top of it. He called the name of that place Beit El, but the name of the city was Luz at the first.

One of the most famous stories in the Tanach that takes place in Beit El is the dream of Yaakov, which has many interpretations. This is a situation that deals with a man who is uprooted from his father's house, penniless, and helpless. He wanders to an unknown future, escorted only with the promise of God, "I shall be with you."

Twenty-two years later, Yaakov returns to Beit El, this time a great man, escorted by his family, large flocks, and possessions, to thank God for being with him in all of his crises; Lavan, Esav, and Shechem.

So Yaakov came to Luz, which is in the land of Canaan – the same is Beit El – he and all the people that were with him. And he built there an altar and called the place El-Beit-El, because there God was revealed to him when he fled from the face of his brother.

There is a very special story about Beit El that takes place many years later during the time of the First Temple.

Following the death of King Shlomo, the huge empire which was built by King David, split into two kingdoms. The kingdom of Yehuda was ruled by Rechavam, son of Shlomo. The other kingdom was ruled by Yerovam, son of Nevat, from the tribe of Efraim.

Yerovam, who is a great man, is appointed by God to be the king of the ten tribes of Israel.

And it came to pass at that time when Yerovam went out of

Jerusalem that the Prophet Achiyah the Shilonite found him in the way. Now Achiyah had clothed himself with a new garment and the two were alone in the field. And Achiyah laid hold of the new garment that was on him and tore it in twelve pieces.

He said to Yerovam: "Take ten pieces for the Lord. The God of Israel said, behold, I will tear the kingdom out of the hand of Shlomo and will give ten tribes to you. But he shall have one tribe for My servant David's sake and for Jerusalem's sake, the city which I have chosen out of all the tribes of Israel.

Yerovam, who has become the king of the ten tribes, thinks to himself...

"Now the kingdom will return to the house of David. If these people will go up to offer sacrifices in the house of the Lord at Jerusalem, then the heart of these people will turn back to their Lord, even to Rechavam, king of Yehuda. And they will kill me, and return to Rechavam king of Yehuda."

The Talmud explains what bothers Yerovam in allowing the people to go to Jerusalem to offer the sacrifices.

According to the Talmud (*Sanhedrin p101*), in the Temple, there were special seats for the kings from the house of David. When the ceremony took place, only the kings from the house of David were allowed to sit. Yerovam thinks to himself, when the ceremony starts, the king of Yehuda, Rechavam, will sit and I will have to stand. People that will see me standing will think that the king is sitting and his servant is standing at his side. If I will try to sit near the king, the people will kill me for sitting in a place that is reserved only for the kings from the house of David.

So the great man, Yerovam, decides to establish a new pagan religion among the ten tribes and make the Jews under his rule worship idols so that they will no longer offer sacrifices in the Temple in Jerusalem.

The king took counsel and made two calves of gold. And he said to them: "You have gone up long enough to Jerusalem.

Behold your gods, O Israel, which brought you up out of the land of Egypt." And he set the one in Beit El and the other put he in Dan.

Next, Yerovam creates a new kind of Kohen, who is not from the tribe of Levi, probably because the Levites would not cooperate with him.

And he made houses of high places and made Kohanim from among all the people that were not of the sons of Levi.

Now Yerovam forms a new major holiday to replace the holiday of Passover, which is celebrated on the fifteenth day of the seventh month.

Yerovam ordained a feast in the eighth month, on the fifteenth day of the month, like the feast that is in Yehuda, and he went up to the altar. So he did in Beit El to sacrifice to the calves that he had made. And he placed in Beit El, the Kohanim of the high places that he had made.

And to make sure that the Jews do not try to go to Jerusalem to offer the original Passover sacrifice to God, Yerovam puts roadblocks on the roads.

And if the roadblocks weren't enough to convince the people to observe the new style of the king's religion, the king himself goes up to the altar to sacrifice to the idol in order to set a good example for the people.

And he went up to the altar which he had made in Beit El on the fifteenth day in the eighth month, even in the month which he had devised of his own heart. And he ordained a feast for the Children of Israel and went up to the altar to offer.

Suddenly, without an invitation, a man from Yehuda appears. And while the king is getting ready for the offering on the new altar, the man turns to the altar and he calls out...

"O altar, altar, said the Lord: Behold, a son shall be born to the house of David, Yoshiyahu by name. And upon you shall he sacrifice the Kohanim of the high places that offer upon you, and men's bones shall they burn upon you."

The appearance of the man and the way he spoke to the altar put everyone into shock. And if this is not enough...

He gave a sign the same day saying: "This is the sign which the Lord has spoken: Behold, the altar shall be split and the ashes that are upon it shall be poured out."

The king is in shock, just like everyone else, yet ...

Yerovam put forth his hand from the altar, saying: "Arrest him."

And now...

His hand, which he put forth against him dried up so that he could not draw it back.

And the sign was seen, as the man says...

The altar also was split and the ashes poured out from the altar according to the sign which the man of God had given by the word of the Lord.

The king, having second thoughts, says...

"Pray now to your God and pray for me that my hand may be restored to me." And the man of God prayed to the Lord and the king's hand was restored to him and became as it was before.

And now the king turns to the man from Yehuda and invites him to his home to eat a meal with him and receive a gift.

But the man of God said to the king: "If you will give me half of your house, I will not go in with you. Neither will I eat bread nor drink water in this place.

So the man from Yehuda leaves, but before he has gone very far, another man from Beit El chases him and asks him to come to his house.

And the man from Yehuda said: "I may not return with you, nor go in with you. Neither will I eat bread nor drink water with you in this place. It was said to me by the word of the Lord: 'You shall eat no bread or drink water there, or turn back to go by the way that you came.'"

And so the man from Beit El lies...

"I also am a prophet as you are. An angel spoke to me by the word of the Lord, saying: 'Bring him back with you into your house, that he may eat bread and drink water.'" – He lied to him.

And so the man from Yehuda joins the man from Beit El to eat and drink.

As they sat at the table, the word of the Lord came to the Prophet that brought him back. He cried to the man of God that came from Yehuda, saying: "Thus said the Lord: 'For as much as you have rebelled against the word of the Lord and have not kept the commandment which the Lord your God commanded you but came back, and have eaten bread and drunk water in the place of which He said to you ...Eat no bread and drink no water. Your carcass shall not come to the grave of your fathers.'"

And so after the meal, the man from Yehuda saddles his donkey and leaves the city to return to Yehuda, but suddenly...

After he left, a lion met him on the way and slew him. His carcass was thrown in the road and the donkey stood by it. The lion also stood by the carcass.

When the story reaches Beit El about the strange picture of a lion sitting next to the carcass of a man, without eating it or his donkey, the man from Beit El, who has been disguised as a prophet, orders his sons to saddle his donkey to go to pick up the carcass of the man from Yehuda.

And the Prophet picked up the carcass of the man of God and laid it on the donkey and brought it back. He came to the city, to lament, and to bury him.

Then he orders his sons...

"When I am dead, bury me in the grave where the man of God is buried. Lay my bones beside his bones.

Why?

For the words which he cried by the word of the Lord against the altar in Beit El, and against all the houses of the high places which are in the cities of the Shomron, shall surely come to pass."

According to the Tanach, *(Kings 2: 23;15)* surely what the man from Yehuda said is now happening by the King of Yehuda, named Yoshiyahu.

Moreover the altar that was at Beit El and the high place which Yerovam, the son of Nevat, who caused Israel to sin, had made, even that altar and the high place he broke down. And he burned the high place and stamped it small to powder and burned the Asherah.

As Yoshiyahu turned himself, he looked at the graves that were there in the mount and he sent and took the bones out of the graves and burned them upon the altar and defiled it, according to the word of the Lord which the man of God said.

Then he said: "What monument is that which I see."

And the men of the city told him: "It is the grave of the man of God, who came from Yehuda and proclaimed these things that you have done against the altar of Beit El."

And he said: "Let him be. Let no man move his bones." So they left his bones alone with the bones of the Prophet that came out of the Shomron.

The Talmud tells us that the name of the man from Yehuda was Edo the Prophet, and the man from Beit El disguised as a Prophet is Yehonatan ben Gershom. *(Bava Batra p109)*

The Talmud further explains that after the event in Beit El where the altar was miraculously destroyed by the word of the Prophet, God turns to Yerovam and says to him that if he will repent now and return to be the great man that he used to be, then David, Yerovam, and God will walk together in Heaven.

According to the Talmud *(Sanhedrin p102)*, Yerovam then asks God who is going to lead. And God answers that it will be David. Yerovam responds to God, "If David will lead, then I am not interested."

After this, Yerovam did not return from his evil way, but made again from among all the people, Kohanim of the high places. Whosoever would, he consecrated him that he might be one of the Kohanim of the high places.

And so we can see that Beit El, which had been named as the House of God by Yaakov, came to be many years later in the time of Yerovam, a leading city for pagan ritual.

Beit El of today is a new settlement which is renewing Jewish existence in the area of ancient Beit El.

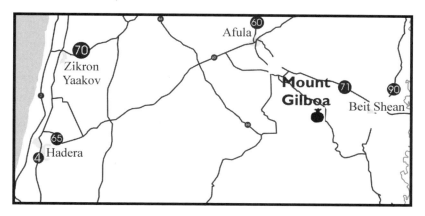

In The Time Of Shaul
Shmuel 1: 28, 31 ~ Shmuel 2: 1

Mount Gilboa

W hen you are standing on top of Mount Gilboa facing north, the valley beneath is built of beautiful squares. Each one grows different kinds of crops. Fish pools can be seen among the fields. In the distance you can see the lush mountains of the Lower Galilee. Turning slightly to the left, Mount Tavor stands proudly in the heart of the Lower Galilee. Far away in front of you, you can see the white snow cap of the highest mountain in Israel, the Herman. Slightly to the right, you can see the city of Beit Shean, located in the middle of the Jordan Valley. On your right, across the Jordan Valley, the Gilad Mountains are blocking the view. This is definitely one of the most beautiful observation points in northern Israel.

Today this view is full of life and activity, unlike the last 2,000 years when this view was of a desolate and swampy region.

At that time, as you can imagine, travelers in their caravans were heading back and forth, and the valley was busy and full of life, almost like today.

Suddenly, a major conflict disturbs the tranquility of the region. The quiet green valley becomes a battlefield between two armies, the army of the invaders, the Philistines, and the army of Israel, who tries to block the intruders.

The Philistines gathered themselves together and came and pitched in Shunem. Shaul gathered all Israel together and they pitched in Gilboa.

Shaul tries to build an army that will face the Philistines, but he has serious difficulties.

First, David, his most important officer, is not with him because the King's jealousy has chased him away. And because David is not with Shaul, the family of David will not join Shaul's army. Without the family of David, which is one of the most important ones in the tribe of Yehuda, he will not have the support of Yehuda. And without Yehuda, many of the other tribes will not feel like they have to be with Shaul either. So Shaul arrives to the battlefield, mostly with his tribe, Benjamin, which is not enough to defeat the strong Philistine army.

Second, Shaul arrives to this battlefield without the spiritual support that he lost from God when he went into battle to destroy Amalek. He was ordered to kill every person and every animal, but failed to listen God's instructions and spared the life of their king and the animals. This angered God and He withdrew His support from Shaul and would not answer him.

Third, the Prophet Shmuel, who is Shaul's most important spiritual leader, dies. Shaul becomes very distressed and feels very alone.

When Shaul saw the camp of the Philistines, he was afraid and his heart trembled greatly.

Shaul is afraid and it bothers him to lead his people into a war when he does not have spiritual guidance.

When Shaul asked the Lord, the Lord did not answer him, neither by dreams, nor by the Urim, nor by prophets.

Shaul is so lost that he turns to his people, asking...

"Find me a woman that practices witchcraft by a ghost, that I may go to her, and inquire of her."

His servants can see how desperate the king is and they help him, even though three weeks before, the king gave an order to kill anyone who practiced witchcraft.

His servants said to him: "Behold, there is a woman that is at Endor."

As darkness fell on the camp that night on Mount Gilboa, Shaul and his servants dress as simple, common people and ride straight to the house of the sorcerer.

Shaul disguised himself and put on common clothes. He went with his two men and they came to the woman by night.

The late night arrival of the three men, who ask...

"Bring me, by a spirit, whomever I shall name to you."

...worries the woman to question...

"You know what Shaul has done, how he has cut off those who divine by a ghost or a familiar spirit out of the land. Why do you lay a trap for my life, to cause me to die?"

And when the man swears to her by God not to cause her harm, she agrees...

"Whom shall I bring up to you?"

And the man says...

"Bring up Shmuel."

When the spirit of Shmuel appears, the woman realizes who this man is.

She cried with a loud voice. The woman spoke to Shaul, saying: "Why have you deceived me? You are Shaul."

Shaul, who has been exposed, answers...

"Don't be afraid. Tell me what you see."

So the terrified woman describes her vision.

"I see a godlike being coming up out of the earth."

Shaul asks...

"What does he look like?"

And the woman says...

"An old man comes. He is covered with a robe."

The description is very clear...

And Shaul understood that this was Shmuel...

Because...

Shmuel's mother made him a little robe and brought it to

The Talmud explains that the meaning of the expression, a *godlike creature coming up out of the earth*, refers to the arrival of Shmuel, together with Moshe. It appears that Shmuel needs spiritual support to face the King of Israel at this crucial moment. *(Hagiga, p4)*

him from year to year, when she came up with her husband to offer the yearly sacrifice.
(Shmuel 1: 2;19)

As the spirit of Shmuel arrives, it turns to Shaul very upset, asking...

"Why have you disturbed me, to bring me up?"

And so the embarrassed king apologizes, saying...

"I am very distressed because the Philistines make war against me and God has departed from me. He does not answer me anymore, neither by prophets, nor by dreams. So I have called you to tell me what I need to do."

The words of Shmuel are sharp as a knife and as cold as ice.

The Midrash explains the technical procedure to bring a spirit and says that the one who brings the spirit can see the spirit, but cannot hear it. And the one who asks for the spirit, can hear it, but cannot see it. (*Vayikra Raba: c26, s7*)

"Why do you ask me, seeing that the Lord has left you and has become your adversary? Because you did not listen to the voice of the Lord, and did not execute His fierce wrath on Amalek, therefore the Lord has done this thing to you this day. The Lord has taken the kingship from your hand and given it to David."

And if that is not enough...

"The Lord will deliver Israel, with you, into the hand of the Philistines."

And...

"Tomorrow you and your sons will be with me."
The message the king hears is devastating.
Shaul fell immediately upon the earth, bowing, and was very afraid.

According to the Midrash, when the terrifying scene finishes, Shaul gets up and his chief of staff, Avner, asks, "What did the Prophet tell you?"

Shaul's answer is definite and clear. "I've been told that tomorrow Israel will overcome the Philistine enemy."

Shaul returns back to the Israeli camp, encouraging his soldiers to fight bravely in the next day's battle because they have been promised victory. That is in spite of the very depressing message he received from Shmuel, that not only will Israel be defeated, but Shaul, together with his sons, will be killed in the war.

Morning comes and the army of Israel marches towards the Philistine army. When the battle begins, quickly it becomes clear that the hand of the Philistines is far stronger.
Now the Philistines fought against Israel. The men of Israel fled from the Philistines and fell dead in Mount Gilboa.

The Israeli soldiers fight desperately against the much stronger Philistine army. And in a short while, the king sees his sons being killed.
The Philistines chased Shaul and his sons. The Philistines slew Yonatan, and Avinadav, and Malchishua, the sons of Shaul.

The king tries to retreat and escape, but...
The battle went against Shaul, and the archers overtook him. He was in great fear from the archers.

The king understands what is about to happen when he falls alive into the hands of the Philistines. Shaul is very concerned about the position of the King of Israel. He does not want to let the Philistines humiliate and abuse the body of the king.

Shaul said to his armor-bearer: "Draw your sword and thrust it into me. Do not let these uncircumcised come and thrust it through me. Do not let them make a mock of me." But his armor-bearer would not, for he was very afraid.

And so...

Shaul took his sword, and fell upon it.

By the end of the day, the horrifying results of the battle become known to everyone. Israel has been defeated. The sons of the king have been killed. And the King of Israel is dead, falling on his own sword.

The Midrash gives us a very special angle to understand the personality of King Shaul.

When the king received the unexpected message that his army would be defeated by the Philistines and that he and his sons would be killed in the battle, Shaul, as the king, could have avoided the battle.

Kings do not have to lead their army. Shaul could send his soldiers and stay behind. But Shaul does not. He encourages his army to fight and defend the name of Israel. So he, with his sons, leads the army.

At this point, according to the Midrash, God turns to His Throne saying, "Look at this man that I have created. He is going to the battle with his sons, knowing he will not return. We all know that a man would not go to the bathhouse with his sons because of the harm of the evil eye, and this man, Shaul, for the name of Israel, is sacrificing himself and his sons."

According to the Midrash, this behavior brought the spirit of Shmuel to say to Shaul, "Tomorrow you and your sons will be with me." *With me* means in Olam Haba (the next world), together with the righteous.

(Vayikra Raba: c26, s7)

On the mountain of Gilboa, one of the most tragic, yet heroic periods of the people of Israel, led by a very unique man, King Shaul, has ended.

The morning after the battle, the Philistines find the body of Shaul. His head is cut off and is taken to be shown in the Philistine cities. His body is stuck on a pole on the wall of the city, Beit Shean.

And it came to pass on the next day, when the Philistines came to strip the slain, that they found Shaul and his three sons fallen in Mount Gilboa. They cut off his head and stripped off his armor and sent it into the land of the Philistines, to carry the news to the house of their idols, and to the people. They put his armor in the house of the Ashtarot and they fastened his body to the wall of Beit Shean.

This is the place to hear the response of David, when he receives the news about the fall of King Shaul and his sons.

Since Shaul considered David to be his enemy and pursued David to kill him, we would expect David to rejoice over the falling of his enemy, but David does not. David reacts bitterly and he mourns the fall of the king.

David took hold of his clothes and tore them. Likewise all the men that were with him. They wailed and wept and fasted until the evening for Shaul, for Yonatan his son, for the people of the Lord, and for the house of Israel because they fell by the sword. (Shmuel 2: 1;11,12)

Then, out of pain and anger, David recites the most powerful lamentation we read in the Tanach, which still echoes on this mountain until today.

David lamented with this lamentation over Shaul and over Yonatan his son and said...

Teach the sons of Yehuda the bow. Behold, it is written in the book of Yashar: Your beauty, O Israel, on your high places is slain! How are the mighty fallen! Tell it not in Gat, publish it not in the streets of Ashkelon. Do not let the daughters of the Philistines rejoice. Do not let the daughters of the uncircumcised triumph.

The mountains of Gilboa, let there be no dew or rain upon you, neither fields of choice fruits, for there the shield of the mighty was vilely cast away, the shield of Shaul, not anointed with oil.

From the blood of the slain, from the fat of the mighty, the bow of Yonatan turned not back and the sword of Shaul returned not empty. Shaul and Yonatan, the lovely and the pleasant in their lives, even in their death, they were not divided. They were swifter than eagles. They were stronger than lions.

Daughters of Israel, weep over Shaul, who clothed you in scarlet and with other delights, who put ornaments of gold upon your apparel.

How are the mighty fallen in the midst of the battle! Yonatan, upon your high places is slain! I am distressed for you, my brother Yonatan. Very pleasant have you been to me. Wonderful was your love to me, passing the love of women.

How are the mighty fallen and the weapons of war perished!

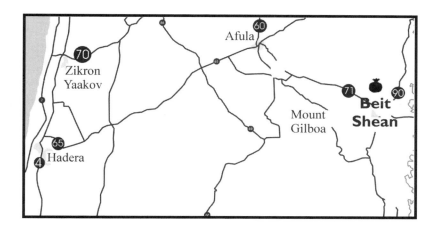

In The Time Of Shaul
Shmuel 1: 11, 31 ~ Judges: 21

Beit Shean

Beit Shean is located at the junction of two valleys
that connects the valley of Yizrael going west and
the Jordan Rift Valley going north to south. The city
is surrounded with a high ridge of mountains from
all directions. Overlooking the city in the east are the Heights
of Gilad and southwest, are the Gilboa Mountains. In the north-
west, are the hills of the Lower Galilee.

The city is on a highway that connects Syria and the
Heights of Gilad to the coast of Israel. The *Tel* (hill) of the
ancient Beit Shean impressively blocks the entrance to the valley and controls the highway.

Water flows from Mount Gilboa and the Jordan River
to the city. For these reasons, Beit Shean has grown into an
important city of commerce, settled for over 4,000 years through
today.

The biblical story that involves Beit Shean is from the
time of King Shaul, a few decades before the First Temple is to
be built.

The battle between Shaul and the Philistines just ended
on Mount Gilboa. Israel has been defeated. Smoke is coming
from burnt villages and cities, which have been conquered by

the Philistines.

When the men of Israel that were on the other side of the valley, and they that were beyond the Jordan, saw that the men of Israel fled, and that Shaul and his sons were dead, they abandoned the cities, and fled. The Philistines came and dwelled in them.

A battlefield in those days and even in our time is a very interesting place which can provide many surprises. The dead bodies left after the battle always leave something precious behind.

And it came to pass on the next day, when the Philistines came to strip the slain, that they found Shaul and his three sons fallen in Mount Gilboa.

And that was a good enough reason for a party for the Philistines.

They cut off his head, stripped off his armor, and sent into the land of the Philistines round about, to carry the news to the house of their idols, and to the people.

The battle gear...

...they put in the house of the Ashtarot.

And the remains of what was left of the body of Shaul...

...they hung up on the wall of Beit Shean.

Now the party begins. Beer and wine is spilled like water. The celebration of victory over the Israelites and the killing of their king and his sons lasts throughout the night.

In the morning, after the effects of the wine have worn off, the Philistines realize that the bodies of the king and his sons have disappeared. They were too drunk to hear or see people from Yavesh-Gilad come and take the bodies.

When the inhabitants of Yavesh-Gilad heard what happened to him, that which the Philistines had done to Shaul, all the brave men arose and went all night and took the body of Shaul and the bodies of his sons from the wall of Beit Shean.

The people of Yavesh-Gilad risk their lives to save whatever is left of the body of Shaul and his sons for two reasons.

One, they owe Shaul because the first battle that Shaul, as a king, conducts is against Nachash the Ammonite, the enemy of Yavesh-Gilad, who threatens to pursue the people to kill them.

It was on the next day that Shaul put the people in three companies. They came into the midst of the camp in the morning watch and smote the Ammonites until the heat of the day. It came to pass that they that remained scattered, so that two of them were not left together.

Two, Shaul is related to the people of Yavesh-Gilad as it is described in the story of the battle of Giva in Judges, chapter 21. By the end of the battle of Israel against Benjamin, only 600 men from Benjamin survive. Because Yavesh-Gilad did not join Israel against Benjamin, the community of Yavesh-Gilad is wiped out, except for 400 girls. Eventually these girls are given as wives to Benjamin and that is how Yavesh-Gilad is related to Shaul.

The congregation sent twelve thousand men of the bravest and commanded them, saying: "Go and smite the inhabitants of Yavesh-Gilad with the edge of the sword, with the women and the little ones. This is what you shall do. You shall utterly destroy every male and every woman that has lain with a man."

They found among the inhabitants of Yavesh-Gilad four hundred young virgins, that had not known man by lying with him. They brought them to the camp at Shilo, which is in the land of Canaan.

Benjamin returned at that time. They gave them the women whom they had saved alive of the women of Yavesh-Gilad.

The people of Yavesh-Gilad, after accomplishing this heroic mission of saving the bodies of the king and his sons, fast for seven days.

They took their bones and buried them under the tamarisk tree in Yavesh and fasted seven days.

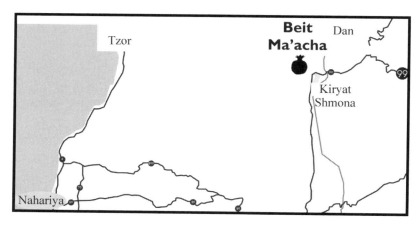

In The Time Of David
Shmuel 2: 10, 12

Tel Avel Beit Ma'acha

On your way from the city of Kiryat Shmona to the small, beautiful town of Metula in the north of Israel, you will enter into a narrow valley, locked between the mountains of Naftali on your left, and Ayun on your right. On top is the border between Israel and Lebanon. The Ayun Valley blooms with orchards of densely planted apples and pears, and escorts the river of Ayun, flowing with fresh cold water.

Behind the valley, a hill shaped like the back of a camel is the very place of our biblical story. The name of the hill, from 3,000 years ago, is Tel Avel Beit Ma'acha.

Tel is a term that means an ancient city was built up and destroyed many times throughout history and now is in ruins and deserted.

The meaning of the term Avel refers to a city that is located on a nice source of water.

Ma'acha is the name of the daughter of the king of Geshur, who named the city, Beit Ma'acha, after his beautiful daughter.

Geshur was known as one of the strong kingdoms in the north of Israel during the time of the First Temple period.

As the king of Israel, David has to deal with the security problems of Israel. One after the other, he has to conquer Israel's neighboring enemy nations.

This story starts when David tries to comfort Hanun, the king of Bnei Ammon, whose father has just died.

The king of the Children of Ammon died and Hanun his son reigned in his place. David said: "I will show kindness to Hanun, the son of Nachash, as his father showed kindness to me."

David pays respect to the dead king by sending a delegation to comfort his son.

David sent, by the hand of his servants, to comfort him concerning his father. And David's servants came into the land of the Children of Ammon.

The advisors of Hanun, king of Ammon have a different opinion about the reason David sends his people.

But the princes of the Children of Ammon said to Hanun their lord: "You think that David does honor to your father, that he sent comforters to you? Has not David sent his servants to you to search the city and to spy it out and to overthrow it?"

Hanun is too young and inexperienced to realize the mistake his advisors are bringing him to.

So Hanun took David's servants and shaved off one half of their beards and cut off their garments to the middle and sent them away.

When David gets the message of what happened to his people...

David sent to meet them for the men were greatly ashamed. And the king said: "Wait at Jericho until your beards are grown and then come back."

Soon afterwards, David discovers that the people of Ammon made arrangements to face his expected attack on them.

When the Children of Ammon saw that they were repugnant to David, the Children of Ammon sent and hired the Arameans of Beit Rechov, and the Arameans of Tzova, twenty thousand soldiers, and the king of Ma'acha with a thousand men, and the men of Tov, twelve thousand men.

And so, David, who went to show respect to the dead king of Ammon, has now found himself fighting all the nations dwelling north and east to Israel.

During the battle against Geshur, David sees the daughter of the king and he falls in love with her.

According to the Talmud, in the first place, David didn't have to show respect to a king who was an enemy of Israel during the period of Judges and Shaul. In the second place, a Jewish king is not supposed to show respect to a pagan king. So God has created circumstances that, instead of having peace, David has to fight all the nations, one after the other, including the kingdom of Geshur. *(Bamidbar Raba 21:5)*

According to the Torah, when a Jewish man takes a woman of the enemy captive during a war, he is not allowed to have her immediately.

When you go to battle against your enemies, and the Lord your God delivers them into your hands, and you carry them away captive, and see among the captives a woman of goodly form, and you have a desire for her, and would take her to be your wife, then you shall bring her home to your house.

The man must wait a month while she is crying for her father's house, being neglected, and losing her beauty.

She shall shave her head and pare her nails. She shall take the clothing of her captivity from off her and shall remain in your house and wail for her father and her mother a full month.

After this month, if he still wants her, he is allowed to have her only as his wife...

After that you may go to her and be her husband. She shall be your wife.

And that is exactly what David does. Poor David falls

in love with Ma'acha and insists on marrying the daughter of the king of Geshur.

David ignores the next issue the Torah deals with, which follow the laws of taking a woman in war. This is the issue of dealing with a disobedient son. The Torah promises that if you insist on marrying a woman captured in a war, you will end up with a son from her who will be disobedient. This is exactly what happens to David.

If a man has a stubborn and rebellious son that will not listen to the voice of his father or the voice of his mother, and though they punish him, he will not listen to them, then his father and his mother shall lay hold on him and bring him out to the elders of his city and to the gate of his place. They shall say to the elders of his city: "This, our son, is stubborn and rebellious. He does not listen to our voice. He is a glutton and a drunkard."

All the men of his city shall stone him with stones, so that he will die. (Devarim 21)

Relations between Ma'acha and David bring Avshalom, who grows to be a most handsome man.

Now in all Israel, there was none to be so much praised as Avshalom for his beauty, from the sole of his foot to the crown of his head. There was no blemish on him.

And Avshalom is very ambitious, to the point that he is ready to kill his father to take his place as king.

The son's disobedience that the Torah promises, does not stop with Avshalom.

Avshalom has a sister named Tamar.

It came to pass after this, that Avshalom, the son of David, had a fair sister, whose name was Tamar. Amnon, the son of David loved her.

Amnon has an original idea to impress Tamar.

Now Amnon rested and played sick. When the king came to see him, Amnon said to the king: "Let my sister Tamar come and make me a couple of cakes in my sight, that I may eat from her hand."

So Tamar is sent to take care of her "sick" brother...

Tamar went to her brother Amnon's house and he was lying down. She took dough and kneaded it and made cakes in his sight and did bake the cakes.

But Amnon quickly ends this game...

When she had brought them near to him to eat, he took hold of her and said to her: "Come lie with me, my sister."

So Tamar says...

"No, my brother. Do not force me for no such thing ought to be done in Israel. Do not do this evil thing."

Because...

"Where shall I carry my shame? As for you, you will be as one of the most despicable men in Israel."

But, there is a way we can be together...

"So speak to the king because he will not withhold me from you."

Amnon's passion has blinded him...

He would not listen to her. Being stronger than her, he forced her and lay with her.

And when Amnon finished everything, suddenly...

Amnon hated her with exceedingly great hatred. The hatred he had for her was greater than the love that he had loved her.

Amnon flipped upside down and now he wants her to disappear.

"Get up and leave."

Tamar begs him...

"Do not do this greater evil than that what you just did to me."

Again, hatred has overtaken Amnon.

He would not listen to her.

Cold as ice...

He called his servant that ministered to him, and said: "Send this one away from me and lock the door after her."

The door is opened...

And his servant took her out and locked the door after her.

Thrown out, abused and humiliated, Tamar leaves the house of Amnon.

Now she had a garment of many colors upon her. With such robes were the king's daughters dressed who were virgins.

At this point, Tamar screams her shame.

Tamar put ashes on her head, and tore her garment of many colors that was on her. And she laid her hand on her head and went her way, crying aloud as she went.

Tamar's brother, Avshalom, takes responsibility for her and tries to help.

Avshalom, her brother, said to her: "Was Amnon, your brother, with you? Now hold your peace, my sister. He is your brother. Take not this thing to heart." So Tamar remained despondent in her brother, Avshalom's house.

The Midrash explains the definition of real love.

If there is something that love depends on, then it is a false love.

If this love does not depend on anything, then it is real love.

The example of real love that the Midrash uses is the relationship between David and Yonatan.

The "great love" Amnon had for Tamar was false as it was based on something Amnon wanted from Tamar. Once he had it, the love disappeared and turned into hatred.
(Yalcut Shimoni, Shmuel 2:149)

Avshalom never reveales any of what he has in his heart towards Amnon. Two years passed and when it looks like the whole story has been forgotten, Avshalom organizes a small celebration in his house. All his brothers are invited.

After two full years, Avshalom had sheep-shearers in Baal Hazor, which is next to Efraim. Avshalom invited all the king's sons.
...including Amnon.
He let Amnon and all the king's sons go with him.

Now Avshalom has not forgotten what Amnon did to his sister, Tamar.

Avshalom commanded his servants, saying: "Be ready when Amnon's heart is full with wine. When I say to you: 'Strike Amnon.' Then kill him and have no fear. Have not I commanded you? Be courageous and be valiant."

When the wine overtakes the people at the party, a sign is given...

The servants of Avshalom did to Amnon as Avshalom had commanded.

The rest of the participants at the bloody party run for their lives...

Then all the kings sons arose. Each man got on his mule and ran away.

Avshalom leaves the scene of the crime. His destination is in the north...

Avshalom fled and went to Talmai, the son of Ammihud, king of Geshur.

Avshalom finds the king of Geshur and the city, named after his mother, Ma'acha, as a refuge where he can safely hide from justice for killing Amnon, his brother. For three years, Avshalom finds Avel Beit Ma'acha as a safe place to live and build his conspiracy against his father, King David.

In The Time Of
David

Avel Beit Ma'acha

Shmuel 2: 19, 20

M
a'acha has the "honor" to be the location for another story recorded in the Tanach. This story
begins right after the end of the first revolt against
King David, conducted by his son, Avshalom,
who dies in a battle in Efraim Forest. The army he gathers
dissipates and King David is asked by Israel to return to Jerusalem and rule the sons of Israel.

All the people were consulting throughout all the tribes of
Israel, saying: "The king delivered us out of the hand of our en-
emies and he saved us out of the hand of the Philistines. Now he
has fled out of the land from Avshalom. And Avshalom, whom we
anointed over us, is dead in battle. Now, therefore, why do you not
speak of bringing the king back?"

The Tanach describes a large delegation from Yehuda
and another delegation from Israel who come to welcome the
king as he returns to his city, Jerusalem.

All the people went over the Jordan. And the king went over.
So the king went over to Gilgal, and Chimham went over with him.
All the people of Yehuda brought the king over, and also half the
people of Israel.

At this point, a senseless argument starts between the

people of Yehuda and the people of Israel. It looks like each one of the groups wants to take the opportunity to show that it is closer to the king. The people of Yehuda manage to surround the king, while the people of Israel are in the outer circle of the king. The people of Israel complain to the king...

"Why have our brothers, the men of Yehuda stolen you away."

The people of Yehuda respond...

"Because the king is related to me. Why are you angry over this matter? Have we eaten at all of the king's cost or has any gift been given us?"

At this point, the argument turns quite vocal and frustrating for Israel...

"We have ten parts in the king. Also, we have more right in David than you."

A typical small political argument takes place in front of our very eyes – Who tried harder to bring back the king – the people of Israel or the people of Yehuda? The winner of this argument hopes to receive seats, budgets, and closer connections to the king and his power.

"Why then did you slight us? Was it not our advice to bring back our king?"

The people of Yehuda technically and by relations, were closer to the king...

And the words of the men of Yehuda were fiercer than the words of the men of Israel.

This frustrating moment for Israel seems like wonderful timing for a man named Sheva ben Bichri.

Now there happened to be there a certain man named Sheva, the son of Bichri, a Benjamite. He blew the shofar and said: "We have no portion in David, neither have we inheritance in the son of Yeshai. Every man to his tents, O Israel."

The people of Israel, uncomfortable, leave the king and return to their places. It is clear that Sheva ben Bichri is about to ride the wave of frustration of the people of Israel to start another revolt against King David.

So all the men of Israel went up from following David and followed Sheva, the son of Bichri. The men of Yehuda did cleave to their king, from the Jordan even to Jerusalem.

Of all the places Sheva ben Bichri decides to start his revolt against David, he chooses the city, Avel Beit Ma'acha.

He went through all the tribes of Israel to Avel, and to Beit Ma'acha, and all the Berites. And they were gathered together and went in also after him.

It looks like Sheva ben Bichri hopes that Avshalom's grandfather, King Geshur, will be a natural ally to host him, to support him, and maybe provide him connections to other potential enemies of David to join him against the king.

David understands that Sheva ben Bichri can cause major damage so he immediately sends his army to finish with the problem Sheva ben Bichri threatened to start.

David said to Avishai: "Now Sheva, the son of Bichri, will do us more harm than did Avshalom! Take your servants and pursue him before he gets the fortified cities to join him before our eyes."

In a short while, the army of David strikes Avel Beit Ma'acha. It is clear that the whole city will be condemned to death for revolting against the king.

But an old, wise woman manages to save the city.

Then cried a wise woman out of the city: "Hear, hear. Say to Yoav: 'Come near that I may speak with you.'"

This woman must be very special to be able to speak this way from the wall.

He came near to her. The woman said: "Are you Yoav?" And he answered: "I am."
Then she said to him: "Hear the words of your handmaid." And he answered: "I do hear."

The woman explains to Yoav that the city is not cooperating with the traitors and the sin of very few people should not be blamed on the rest of the city who know nothing about the reason of the battle.

Then she spoke, saying: "They wanted to speak in old time, saying: They shall surely ask counsel at Avel. So they ended the matter."

And here she introduces herself to be...

...the peaceable and faithful in Israel. Do you seek to destroy a city and a mother in Israel? Why will you swallow up the inheritance of the Lord?"

Yoav responds...

"Far be it, far be it from me that I should swallow up or destroy. The matter is not so, but a man of the hill country of Efraim, Sheva, the son of Bichri by name, has lifted up his hand against the king, even against David. Deliver him only and I will depart from the city."

This woman's expertise was probably in negotiation because the Midrash (*Beresheet Raba c94, s9*) says she managed to convince the people of the city to do something almost impossible, to give the head of Sheva ben Bichri to Yoav.

How did she do it?

The Midrash explains that after the first meeting with Yoav, she went back to the city informing them that Yoav's intention was to level the city and kill everyone in it as traitors.

After the second meeting with Yoav, she returned back to the city, saying, "I was able to convince Yoav to kill only one thousand men."

And after the third meeting, she returned back to the terrified city saying, "All that we need to do is give the head of Sheva ben Bichri." So, the people cooperated with her.

And they cut off the head of Sheva the son of Bichri, and threw it out to Yoav. And he blew the shofar. They were dispersed from the city, every man to his tent. And Yoav returned to Jerusalem to the king.

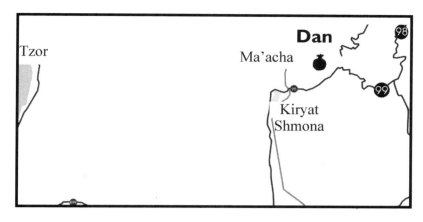

In The Time Of The Judges
Judges: 18 ~ Kings 1: 12

Dan

Whoever looks for a green, lush piece of land, rich with water in Israel probably will be able to find it near the Jordan River. The Jordan River's sources come from three springs. One is the spring coming from the cave where the temple of the idol Pan used to be. Around this spring, a city was built by King Herod, called Panias. The Arabs, who could not pronounce the "P" sound, called it Banias.

The second source comes from the spring of the Hatzbani, which is located on the western slopes of Mount Herman. Around it a Jewish city was built during the time of Yehoshua, called Hatzbaya. This community lasted throughout history until 100 years ago. The Jews of Hatzbaya were known as very strong big-proportioned people who, uniquely for Jews, would hire themselves out as mercenaries.

One hundred years ago, this community was helped by the legendary Rothschild to abandon their settlement because of a war between the Druse and the Marons, who threatened to put this community in danger. These people kept their name Hatzbani wherever they went. Even today, if you meet any of them, you'll find out that they are very big and strong people.

The third water source is the Dan. This spring comes

from the bottom of the hill of the Tel of the city Dan. This city was excavated and found to be the very city the Tanach describes in the book of Judges in chapter 18 as a city that was conquered by the people of Dan and renamed after the father of the tribe, Dan.

In those days there was no king in Israel. These are the days the people of Dan are looking for a place to settle in, because until this day, this tribe had no rest among the tribes of Israel.

The people of Dan urgently look for land to replace their portion that had been given to them by Yehoshua. The need to leave their land becomes imperative after Shimshon is killed by the Philistines.

The people of Dan have difficulties with their neighbors in the west, but when Shimshon dies, the tribe is terrified of the revenge the Philistines are going to take because of what Shimshon did for 20 years to the Philistines.

The Children of Dan sent from their family five men from their whole number, men of valor, from Zorah, and from Eshtaol, to spy out the land and to search it. They said to them: "Go, search the land."

These five men, who were from the best of the tribe, follow the order and make their way to Maale Levona, where they find spiritual support with the idol of Micha and his Kohen, Yehonatan ben Gershom, the grandson of Moshe.

From Maale Levona, they continue their research journey and they arrive...

To Laish and saw the people that were there, how they lived in security, after the manner of the Zidonians, quiet and secure. There was no one in the land with authority that might bother them. They were far from the Zidonians and had no dealings with any man.

The most important thing the five men notice about the city Laish is that this city is totally isolated from the whole area around. This means that the people in the city are not related to any other city and are not connected by defense agreements with any other nation.

The five men return back to the tribe and say...

"Arise and let us go up against them. We have seen the land and it is very good, yet you stand still? Do not be lazy. Go and possess the land. When you go, you shall come to a people secure. The land is large, for God has given it into your hand, a place where there is no want. It has everything that is in the earth."

The tribe packs up and starts marching – men, women, infants, elders – everybody, escorted by...

...six hundred men girt with weapons of war...

...leaving behind an entire land which is going to be taken by the Philistines.

When the tribe arrives in Maale Levona...

The five men that went to spy out the country of Laish asked: "Do you know that there is in these houses an ephod and teraphim, and a graven image and a molten image? Now therefore, you know what to do."

Then 600 men surround the house and Micha is convinced quietly and quickly to cooperate with the people of Dan.

When they went into Micha's house and took the graven image of the ephod and the teraphim and the molten image, the Kohen said to them: "What are you doing?"

They said to him: "Be quiet. Lay your hand on your mouth and come with us, to be a father and a Kohen to us. Is it better for you to be a Kohen to the house of one man or to be a Kohen to a tribe and a family in Israel?"

Silently, the convoy proceeds on its way, with one change.

So they turned and departed. They put the little ones and the cattle and the goods before them.

They were ready for any surprises.

They were a distance away from the house of Micha and

the men that were in the houses near Micha's house were gathered together and overtook the Children of Dan.

But 600 very determined armed men block any option.

Micha saw that they were too strong for him, so he turned and went back to his house.

The Hebrew meaning of the name Laish is lion.

This helps us to understand that the area of Dan's new home used to be like a jungle where wild animals, including lions, lived.

The tribe arrives to the city Laish in total surprise.

They came to Laish, to a people quiet and secure, and killed them with the edge of the sword. They burned the city with fire.

Later on, a new city is built.

They built the city and lived there. They called the name of the city Dan, after the name of Dan their father, who was born to Israel, but the name of the city was Laish at first.

One of the first things the people of Dan do as they start living in the city is to...

...set up for themselves the graven image. Yehonatan, the son of Gershom, the son of Menashe, he and his sons were Kohanim to the tribe of Dan until the day of the exile from the land.

From the time that the city of Dan was established, the tribe of Dan was known to be the closest to idol-worshiping among all the tribes of Israel.

When Yerovam becomes the first king of the ten tribes, after the split between Yehuda and Israel, Yerovam thinks...

"Now the kingdom will return to the house of David."

Yerovam believes that the people of Israel will go to offer sacrifices in the Temple in Jerusalem and the heart of the people will go after the king of Jerusalem.

Then the king advised to make two calves of gold. He said to them: "You have gone up enough to Jerusalem. These are your gods, O Israel, which brought you up out of the land of Egypt."
These idols are stationed in central places...
He set one in Beit El, and the other he put in Dan.

Even today, we can see the actual stage where the idol of Micha and later the golden calf of Yerovam were set up in front of the entrance of the gate on the Tel of Dan.

The story of the city of Dan reflects once again the main problem of the period of the Judges. The tribes of Israel are not only split, but also fall to a very low spiritual level when the influence of the pagan culture of the neighboring nations is able to penetrate into the ritual ceremonies of the Israelites.

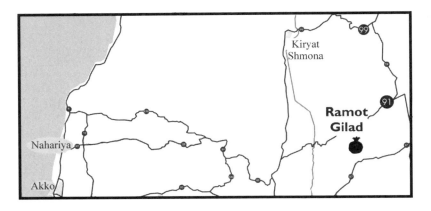

In The Time Of The Kings
Kings 1: 22

Ramot Gilad

The southern part of the Golan Heights is believed to be what the Tanach calls Ramot Gilad. This area, during the time of the kings of Israel, was for a while under the control of the nation of Aram.

Originally this area was settled by the tribes of Gad, Reuven, and half of Menashe when the Israelites entered the Land under the leadership of Yehoshua. This land was known as very good for grazing flocks and other agricultural crops.

During the 1967 War, Israel liberated the Golan Heights, settled it, developed it, and made it into one of the most beautiful areas in Israel.

Almost 3,000 years ago, this was the destination for two armies.

So the king of Israel and Yehoshafat, the king of Yehuda, went up to Ramot Gilad.

The two armies prepare for battle. As the war drums are beating, the king of Israel, Achav, all of a sudden, gets worried.

"What if the prophecy he just heard from the Prophet Michayu comes true and he dies?" thinks King Achav.

And so...

The king of Israel said to Yehoshafat: "I will disguise myself and go into the battle. But you put on your royal robes."

The meaning of this request is that Achav, the king of Israel, will be dressed like a common soldier in order not to be identified, while the king of Yehuda, Yehoshafat will be dressed as a king.

And the king of Israel disguised himself and went into the battle.

Obviously, Achav is very afraid of getting hurt in this battle.

When the battle begins, the king of Aram commands his officers...

"Fight neither with small nor great, seek only the king of Israel."

Following the instructions of the king of Aram, his officers manage to surround King Yehoshafat, thinking that he is Achav, the king of Israel.

When the captains of the chariots saw Yehoshafat, they said: "Surely it is the king of Israel." They turned aside to fight against him...

When Yehoshafat realizes that he is surrounded by the officers of Aram, he turns to God and starts to pray...

Yehoshafat cried out.

The officers of Aram see Yehoshafat praying and so it is clear to them that he is not the king of Israel. They knew that Achav, the king of Israel, would not pray under any circumstances.

When the captains of the chariots saw that it was not the king of Israel, they turned back from pursuing him.

During the chaos of the battle, suddenly...

A certain man drew his bow aimlessly, and struck the king of Israel between the lower armor and the breastplate.

According to the Midrash *(Yalcut Shimoni, Parshat Vaera c183, s8)*, the man who is responsible for hitting the king

According to the Talmud, Yehoshafat is supposed to die at this point. His prayer saves him from sure death and gives him another seven years of life.

The Talmud shows in Chronicles 2 that there are seven years missing from the number of years Yehoshafat actually ruled Yehuda, yet his son Yehoram has seven years more. The Talmud explains that these seven years given to Yehoram were actually the extra years given to Yehoshafat for his prayer during the battle. *(Tosefta Sota c12, s2)*

of Israel and bringing victory to the army of Aram is a common soldier, a leper, and he did it by mistake.

This means that all the effort Achav put into avoiding getting hurt does not help because the man who eventually strikes him is the least expected to do it – a common soldier, a leper, who does it by mistake.

He said to the driver of his chariot: "Turn your hand and carry me out of the camp, for I am wounded."

Achav, in spite of his serious injury, continues to stand in his chariot the entire day of fighting, in order not to discourage the army of Israel.

As the battle intensified that day against Aram, the king was propped up in his chariot.

His blood spills into the chariot for the rest of the day. By the end of the day, Achav collapses...

And he died in the evening. His blood ran out of the wound into the bottom of the chariot.

The Talmud *(Moed Katan, p28)* takes this story as a credit to Achav in that he would not leave the war because of his injury and would stand all day encouraging the soldiers to fight in the name of Israel.

But in the evening...

There went a cry throughout the camp about the going down of the sun, saying: "Every man to his city and every man to his country."

The dead king is brought to Shomron...

So the king died and was brought to Shomron. They buried the king in Shomron. And they washed the chariot by the pool of Shomron and the dogs licked up his blood. The harlots also washed themselves there, according to the word of the Lord, which He spoke.

On the Golan Heights, the career of King Achav has come to an end. The man who was known as one of the most pagan kings of Israel, who followed the evil ways of his wicked wife Ezevel, died trying to fight both the Arameans by trying to liberate Ramot Gilad and at the same time, fighting God.

Prophet Michayahu warned him, "You will not return alive from this battle because of what you did to Navot."

Thus says the Lord: "Have you killed and also taken possessions? In the place where dogs licked the blood of Navot, dogs shall lick your blood also." (Kings 1: 21;19)

And so it was that the death of Achav, on the Golan Heights, was declared in the vineyard of Navot in Yizrael.

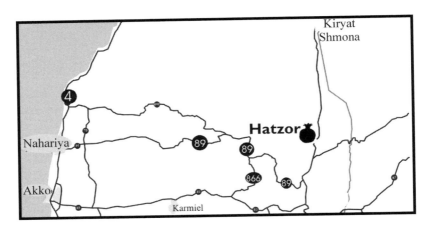

In The Time Of The Judges
Yehoshua: 12 ~ Judges: 4, 5

Hatzor

When you travel from the south of the "finger of Galilee," from Rosh Pinah north on Route 90, you will see on your left, as you cross the riverbed of Hatzor, a very impressive tall hill. This is the *Tel* of the ancient city of Hatzor.

Almost 3,000 years ago, this city was known as one of the most powerful cities in the land of Canaan. During different periods of time, Hatzor was strong enough to control the entire region.

Hatzor held its power because of its location. It was situated very comfortably on the highway that connected the Egyptian empire in the west to the eastern empire on the rivers, Tigris and Euphrates.

Any transportation, any trade, any army activity, needed to cross the city of Hatzor and use its services. This fueled the economy and supported the military power's domination of the region.

When Yehoshua enters into the Land of Israel, he lists the cities and kings he conquers, among them the king of Hatzor.

These are the kings of the land whom Yehoshua and the Children of Israel smote beyond the Jordan westward, from Baal Gad in the valley of Lebanon to the bare mountain, that goes up to Seir. Yehoshua gave it to the tribes of Israel for a possession ac-

cording to their divisions.

The king of Madon, one. The king of Hatzor, one.

The king of Tirzah, one. All the kings, thirty and one.

Yehoshua conquers the land and settles the people of Israel, each tribe in its place according to the *Urim V'tumim*, which signed the precise border between each tribe.

After the death of Yehoshua, Israel enters into the period of Judges, which lasts about 400 years until the time of Kings.

During the time of the Judges, the people of Israel manage on a tribal basis, which means every tribe runs itself. Rarely can we find a Judge who manages to run all Israel as one unit. In those days, the Tanach keeps telling us that whenever Israel forgot God, enemies arrived and started to pursue the people of God.

In the book of Judges in chapter four, we find it again.

And the Children of Israel again did wrong in the eyes of the Lord, after Ehud died.

So...

The Lord gave them over to the hand of Yavin, king of Canaan, who reigned in Hatzor. His captain of the army was Sisera, who lived in Haroshet HaGoim.

Sisera's army was well equipped and the Israelites were afraid.

The Children of Israel cried to the Lord because he had nine hundred chariots of iron.

It took 20 years until Israel turned to God for help.

For twenty years he strongly oppressed the Children of Israel.

In order to show the importance of unity in Israel, God turns to Devorah, a woman living in the area between the two cities, Rama and Beit El, which are quite far from the center of events happening in the north.

Devorah, a Prophetess, the wife of Lapidot, judged Israel

at that time.

Devorah is a smart and very helpful woman. People come to see her and ask for blessings, advice, and help. She meets the people outdoors under a palm tree in order to keep modest relations with them.

She sat under the palm tree of Devorah, between Rama and Beit El in the hill country of Efraim. The Children of Israel came up to her for judgment.

Devorah sends for Barak ben Avinoam, a simple, common man to come to her. He comes from the tribe of Naftali, which is known as a simple tribe.

According to the Midrash, the source of name of Devorah's husband, Lapidot, comes from a custom she had. Devorah would send her husband with torches she made to light the roads to the Mishkan in Shilo at night so that it would be easier and safer to travel.

That's why the people started to call Devorah's husband Lapidot. In Hebrew, Lapidot means torches. *(Yalcut Shimoni, c42)*

She sent and called Barak, the son of Avinoam out of Kedesh Naftali, and said to him: "Has not the Lord, the God of Israel, commanded, saying: 'Go toward Mount Tavor. Take with you ten thousand men of the Children of Naftali and of the Children of Zevulun? I will lead to you to the brook Kishon Sisera, the captain of Yavin's army, with his chariots and his army. I will deliver him into your hand.'"

Barak is not ready for this kind of responsibility. First, because he is coming from a very simple place and second, he is not so sure he can handle this big task.

Barak said to her: "If you will go with me, then I will go. But if you will not go with me, I will not go."

Devorah can tell that Barak suffers from a lack of faith,

so she promises...

"I will surely go with you, but the glory of the battle will not be yours, because the Lord will give Sisera into the hand of a woman." And Devorah arose and went with Barak to Kedesh.

Barak manages to draft 10,000 men from the tribes of Zevulun and Naftali

Barak called Zevulun and Naftali together to Kedesh and there went up ten thousand men at his feet. And Devorah went up with him.

From the top of the mountain of Tavor, Devorah and Barak, and the 10,000 men, could see the army of Sisera very clearly.

Sisera gathered together all his chariots, nine hundred chariots of iron, and all the people that were with him, from Haroshet HaGoim to the brook Kishon.

Iron chariots in the those days were considered to be like tanks in our time. The chances of Barak and his 10,000 men do not look so good, especially when you see the chariots and the huge crowd of men getting prepared for the battle. The situation looks even worse when you know that the army of Sisera is supported by other kings and their armies, who join voluntarily.

But spiritual Devorah can see a different reality.

Devorah said to Barak: "Up. This is the day in which the Lord will deliver Sisera into your hand. Has not the Lord gone out before you?"

To go down straight to the hands of the armies waiting at the bottom of the mountain needs courage.

So Barak went down from Mount Tavor and ten thousand men after him.

The Tanach does not describe in detail what happened...

The Lord caused panic for Sisera and all his chariots and all his army by the edge of the sword before Barak.

Something strange happens which causes the huge army

of Sisera to fall into chaos. Suddenly from the blue sky, a heavy storm of rain hits the valley and the army with the powerful chariots gets stuck in the mud without any ability to move. Even today, the soil of the valley under Mount Tavor can easily turn to a very deep heavy mud when it rains.

Terrifying fear is spread by God. The soldiers of Sisera flee in every direction. Immediately after the storm, an enormous flood carries away what is left of the army and turns the whole battle picture upside down. Barak is left with a very easy job to finish.

But Barak pursued after the chariots and after the army to Haroshet HaGoim. All the army of Sisera fell by the edge of the sword. There was not a man left.

Even the Chief of Staff tries to escape.

Sisera got out of his chariot and fled away on foot.

There is one little hope that Sisera has to help him avoid the destiny of his army.

Sisera fled away on foot to the tent of Yael, the wife of Hever the Kenite. There was peace between Yavin, the king of Hatzor and the house of Hever the Kenite.

It is not usual that a woman would come out of her tent to welcome a strange man, but...

Yael came out to meet Sisera and said to him: "Turn in my lord, turn to me. Fear not." And he turned to her to the tent and she covered him with a blanket.

The tired and thirsty man asks for water, but she gives him milk.

He said to her: "Give me, please, a little water to drink for I am thirsty." But she opened a bottle of milk and gave him drink and covered him.

The man feels safe and secure. Sisera does not know that this command is going to be the last that he will give.

He said to her: "Stand in the door of the tent and it shall be when any man comes and inquires of you, and says: 'Is there any man here? You will say: No.'"

Yael, after her display of wisdom, shows her courage.

Yael, Hever's wife, took a tent pin and took a hammer in her hand. She went softly to him and hit the pin into his temples. It pierced through into the ground. He was in a deep sleep, tired to death.

Barak arrives to the tent, ready to give the final knock-out to his enemy, when...

Yael came out to meet him and said to him: "Come and I will show you the man whom you seek." And he came to her and behold, Sisera lay dead. The tent pin was in his temples.

Imagine the shameful feeling of Barak when he sees that a weak woman did what he was supposed to do.

And this is where the words of Devorah come true when she said to Barak, "If you are not a man to go on your own, the honor of the battle will be given to a woman."

"The glory of the battle will not be yours because the Lord will give Sisera into the hand of a woman."

As the battle ends, Devorah the Prophetess, out of happiness and appreciation to God, sings a most beautiful song praising God for the unbelievable victory. This song can be found in the book of Judges, chapter 5.

Because of the location of Hatzor, this city continued to be an important city for a very long time. King Shlomo turned it into a central city in the north. He built stables for his horses, storage rooms for food, palaces and a very impressive water system which provided for the city in times of emergencies.

Together with the rest of the country when Israel was conquered in 70 *CE*, Hatzor was destroyed and for almost 2,000 years lay in ruins. In the late 1940s, a new kibbutz was founded very close to the Tel called Ayelet HaShahar. The ancient city was excavated by the archeologist Yigal Yadin during the 1960s. Today this is one of the most important archeological sites in northern Israel. The archeological finds from the site are displayed in a museum at the kibbutz, Ayelet HaShahar.

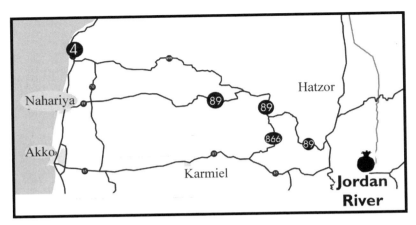

In The Time Of The Kings
Kings 2:5

Jordan River

What is known today as Syria, in the time of the Kings, was the hostile country of Aram. Quite similar to what we know and experience today, constant clashes took place between the kingdom of Israel and Aram. In one of these confrontations...

Aram had gone out in bands and taken captive out of the land of Israel a young girl...

The commander of the army of Aram is a man named Naaman.

She served Naaman's wife.

When the young Israelite girl realizes that Naaman, her master, is a leper...

She said to her mistress: "If my lord will beg before the Prophet that is in Shomron, then he would heal him of his leprosy."

The advice of the young Israelite girl made its way to the king of Aram, so the king sends Naaman with a letter to the king of Israel...

"Go now and I will send a letter to the king of Israel." He departed and took with him ten talents of silver and six thousand pieces of gold and ten changes of clothes. He brought the letter to the king of Israel, saying: "When this letter comes to you, behold, I

have sent Naaman my servant to you, that you may cure him of his leprosy."

Political misunderstandings happen today and definitely happened in those days. The king of Aram meant that the king of Israel should send Naaman to the Prophet to be cured.

But...

When the king of Israel read the letter, he rent his clothes and said: "Am I God, to kill or to give life, that this man sends to me to cure a man of his leprosy? See how he seeks a reason to fight against me."

Elisha the Prophet realizes the misunderstanding...

"Why have you rent your clothes? Let him come to me and he shall know that there is a Prophet in Israel."

The picture now being shaped is that the highest-ranking officer in the army of Aram finds himself in the middle of a misunderstanding between the two kings. Not only that a man in Naaman's high position should be officially escorted, but instead, he has to find his way, alone, to the city of Shomron. There, when he finds the house of the Prophet Elisha, nobody invites him in or gives him the kind of respect and honor due a man of his status.

So Naaman came with his horses and with his chariots and stood at the door of the house of Elisha.

And the rudest way Naaman could be treated is when...

Elisha sent a messenger to him, saying: "Go and wash in the Jordan seven times, and your flesh shall come back to you. You shall be clean."

This was too much...

Naaman was enraged and went away, saying: "Behold, I thought he will surely come out to me and stand and call on the name of the Lord his God, and wave his hand over the place and cure the leper."

Not only was Naaman not treated in the manner for a man of his level, but the Prophet did not even bother to come out of his house to see him and ask him about his disease or call God to show any kind of care for him.

But to send him to immerse in the Jordan River?

"Are not Amanah and Pharpar, the rivers of Damascus, better than all the waters of Israel? May I not wash in them and be clean?" So he turned and went away in a rage.

On his way back home, Naaman starts building plans to take revenge on the Israelites who have just humiliated him.

As he is about to cross the Jordan River on his way back to Damascus...

His servants came near and spoke to him, saying: "My father, if the Prophet had told you to do something great, would you not have done it? How much so then, when he said to you: 'Wash, and be clean?'"

Naaman thinks there is nothing to lose. If it isn't going to help, it isn't going to help.

Then he went down and dipped himself seven times in the Jordan, according to the saying of the man of God. His flesh came back like the flesh of a little child and he was clean.

His anger and rage changed to gratitude and admiration.

He returned to the man of God, he and all his company. He came and stood before him and he said: "Behold now, I know that there is no God in all the earth, but in Israel. Now therefore, please take a present from your servant."

Elisha has no doubts...

But he said: "As the Lord lives, before whom I stand, I will receive none."

And he urged him to take it, but he refused.

The change in Naaman's life reflects in a very unusual request.

"If not, please let there be given to your servant two mules' burden of earth. For your servant will, from now on, offer neither a burnt-offering nor sacrifice to other gods, but only to the Lord."

And another thing...

"The Lord will pardon your servant. When my master goes into the temple of Rimmon to worship there and he leans on my hand and I prostrate myself in the temple of Rimmon, when I prostrate myself in the temple of Rimmon, the Lord will pardon your servant of this."

And now, Naaman, the chief of staff of Aram, leaves.

And he said to him: "Go in peace." So he departed from him a short way.

During the entire dialog between Elisha and Naaman, there is another set of greedy eyes present

Gehazi, the servant of Elisha the man of God, said to himself: "Behold, my master has spared this Naaman the Aramean, in not accepting from his hands what he brought. As the Lord lives, I will surely run after him and take something from him."

Going out in a fast chase, Gehazi is not unnoticed.

Naaman saw someone running after him. He got out of the chariot to meet him and said: "Is all well?"

How is it that the chief of staff of Aram is a leper? — Was there no way to find someone else? The Midrash explains this in Bamidbar Raba.

The event that caused Naaman the leper to be promoted to the rank of chief of staff of Aram was in the battle on Ramot Gilad (the Golan Heights) when he shot the arrow, by mistake, that killed Achav, the king of Israel. *(c7,s5)*

Now Naaman, captain of the host of the king of Aram, was a great man with his master, and held in esteem, because by him the Lord had given victory to Aram. He was also a mighty man of valor, but he was a leper.

(Kings 2, c5, v1)

Heavily breathing, Gehazi explains...

"All is well. My master has sent me, saying: 'Just now from the hill country of Efraim, two young men of the sons of the Prophet have come. Give them, please, a talent of silver and two changes of clothes.'"

Naaman responds, "By all means...

"Be content. Take two talents." And he urged him and bound two talents of silver in two bags with two changes of clothes. He laid them upon two of his servants and they carried them before him.

After the silver and the clothing have been safely hidden by Gehazi...

He went in and stood before his master.

The Prophet looks like he is in a vision when suddenly he asks...

"Where are you coming from, Gehazi?"

Innocent, like a pure lamb, Gehazi answers...

"Your servant went nowhere."

But a prophet is a prophet. He sees things...

"Did my heart not go with you, when the man turned back from his chariot to meet you? Is this a time to receive money, and to receive garments, and oliveyards and vineyards, and sheep and oxen, and men servants and maid servants?"

So it is a package deal for Gehazi...

"The leprosy of Naaman shall cleave to you and to your children forever." And he went out from his presence a leper as white as snow.

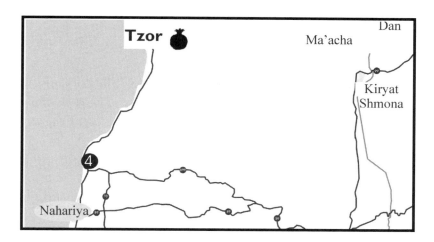

In The Time Of The Kings
Kings 1, 17

Tzor

Tzor is the place where God will convince Eliyahu to bring back the rain, which he stopped in Jericho, as a result of the idol worship of King Achav.

When Eliyahu shows God that he is blind to the suffering of the people who have had no rain for three years, God sends His Prophet to Zarefat, which is today Tzor, saying...

"Arise, go to Zarefat, which belongs to Zidon. Dwell there. I have commanded a widow there to support you."

Eliyahu has no idea what God is planning for him.

So he arose and went to Zarefat. When he came to the gate of the city, a widow was there gathering sticks. He called to her and said: "Get me, please, a little water in a vessel so that I can drink." As she was going to get it, he called to her and said: "Bring me, please, some bread."

Eliyahu's request is so strange. Hasn't he heard about the hunger that has spread in the land?

And she said: "As the Lord your God lives, I have not a cake, only a handful of meal in the jar and a little oil in the cruse. I am gathering two sticks so that I may go in and dress it for me and my son, that we may eat it, and die."

Eliyahu promises the woman...

"Do not fear. Go and do as I said. Make me a little cake

first and bring it to me. Afterwards, make for you and for your son for thus says the Lord, the God of Israel: 'The jar of meal shall not be finished off. Neither shall the cruse of oil lack, until the day that the Lord sends rain to the land.'"

As Eliyahu said...

The jar of meal was not finished off. Neither did the cruse of oil lack, according to the word of the Lord, which He spoke to Eliyahu.

Eliyahu lives in the home of the widow and she provides for his needs until...

The son of the woman, the lady of the house, became sick. His sickness was so bad that there was no breath left in him.

When the woman's son dies, out of pain, she turns to Eliyahu blaming him.

"What have I to do with you, O man of God? Did you come to me to mention my sin and to kill my son?"

The words of the widow hurt Eliyahu badly.

He said to her, "Give me your son." He took him out of her bosom and carried him up into the attic, where he lived, and laid him on his own bed.

Offended, Eliyahu turns to God complaining...

"O Lord my God, have You also brought evil upon the widow with whom I

The Talmud explains God's whole purpose in bringing Eliyahu to Zarefat.

When Eliyahu asks for the life of the son of the widow, God says, "You already have the key of the rain. Now you are asking for the key of life. No one can have two keys. If you want the key of life, you must return the key of rain."

Now Eliyahu understands that he has been trapped by God to bring back the rain. He has no choice and agrees. *(Sanhedrin, p113) am staying to kill her son?"*

Eliyahu knows what he has to do.

So he stretches himself on the child three times and cries to the Lord and says: "O Lord my God, please let this child's soul come back into him."

The Lord listened to the voice of Eliyahu. The soul of the child came back into him and he revived.

As Eliyahu carries the boy back to his mother, he starts planning...

Eliyahu took the child and brought him down into the house and returned him to his mother. Eliyahu said: "See, your son is alive."

The woman said to Eliyahu: "Now I know that you are a man of God and that the word of the Lord in your mouth is truth."

Eliyahu figures out how to make Achav repent before he brings back the rain.

Eliyahu is a zealot and he will not give up without a real fight. The battle now is to make Achav repent. He doesn't have a lot of time, because he promises to bring back the rain, so it must be done quickly.

How Eliyahu navigates his way to bring the king of Israel to repent will be found in the story of Mount Carmel.

According to the Midrash, the son of the widow from Zarefat grows up to be a man who follows Eliyahu and becomes one of his disciples. The boy's name is Yona.

An entire book of Tanach, Yona, tells a story that is so important that Jews read it every year during the afternoon service of Yom Kippur – the holiest day of the year.

One of Yona's deeds was to anoint Yehu ben Nemshi as king of Israel. It is Yehu who wipes out Achav and Ezevel's family – Eliyahu's bitter enemy for many years. *(Rabba)*

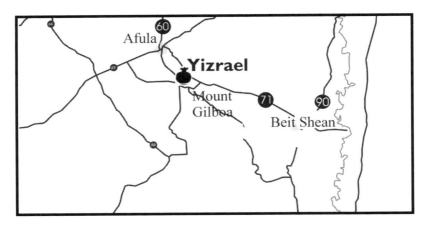

In The Time Of The Kings
Kings 1: 21, 22 ~ Kings 2: 9

Yizrael

One of the most beautiful, fertile valleys in Israel is the valley of Yizrael (Jezreel), whose name comes from the name of a city that was located on its southern edge.

Today, the valley of Yizrael is the scene of another heroic story of the enormous pioneering effort invested to turn this valley from an unmarchable swampy area into the beautifully cultivated area we see today.

Looking down from the hill of Tel Yizrael we see a very impressive site. Squares and squares of beautifully cultivated soil, with all kinds of crops. From grain to vegetables, flowers and fish ponds surround the communities living in the valley.

The city of Yizrael 3,000 years ago was the summer capital of the kingdom of the ten tribes of Israel.

The Tanach tells us a story about King Achav. One day Achav goes out to his balcony, overlooking the valley, and realizes that a most beautiful vineyard grows not so far from his palace. The vineyard is so nice that the king decides to inquire who the owner is in order to buy it.

Achav spoke to Navot, saying: "Give me your vineyard so that I may have it for a garden of herbs because it is near my house. I will give you a better vineyard than this one or, if it seems good to you, I will give you the value of it in money."

Navot is neither ready to sell nor to exchange this land, saying "the land this vineyard is planted on belonged to my grandfather, who died already, and will belong to my grandson, who has not yet been born. This land is my family's property and I cannot trade it or sell it for any price.

Navot said to Achav: "The Lord forbids me that I should give the inheritance of my fathers to you."

But Achav cannot stand being rejected, so...

He came into his house sullen and displeased because of what Navot the Yizraeli had spoken to him. He had said: "I will not give you the inheritance of my fathers." And he laid him down upon his bed and turned away his face and would eat no bread.

Achav's wife, Ezevel, who is known as very ambitious and talented comes to him and says...

"Why is your spirit so sullen, that you eat no bread?"

So Achav tells her about Navot's refusal to sell him the vineyard.

His wife, Ezevel said to him: "Do you now govern the kingdom of Israel? Get up and eat bread. Let your heart be merry."

Because...

"I will give you the vineyard of Navot the Yizraeli."

Ezevel is quite surprised about the way Achav governs Israel, that even a vineyard he wants, he cannot get. So she decides to show him a lesson in rulership and uses one of her methods of getting what she wants.

She wrote letters in Achav's name and sealed them with his seal. She sent the letters to the elders and to the nobles that were in his city and that lived with Navot.

The idea is very simple. Two of her servants will become witnesses, by her order, that Navot cursed the king.

She set two men, bad fellows, before him, and let them bear witness against him, saying: "You did curse God and the king."

The court has no other choice but to sentence Navot to death...

"Carry him out and stone him, that he die."

According to Jewish law, a man who curses the king should die and his possessions will go to the king.

When Ezevel heard that Navot was stoned and was dead, Ezevel said to Achav: "Get up, take possession of the vineyard of Navot the Yizraeli, which he refused to give you for money. For Navot is not alive, but dead."

Achav is not asking any questions like, "How did you do this? What was the cost?"

When Achav heard that Navot was dead, he rose up to go down to the vineyard of Navot the Yizraeli, to take possession of it.

So simple, so easy, and nobody knows anything. Nobody asks any questions. Almost the perfect crime. But yet there is one problem. God knows what happened and is upset.

The word of the Lord came to Eliyahu the Tishbi, saying: "Arise, go down to meet Achav, king of Israel, who dwells in Shomron. He is in the vineyard of Navot, where he has gone down to take possession of it."

God is not happy that Achav does not even ask how the vineyard came into his possession. So God asks...

"Have you killed and also taken possessions?"

And then God says...

"In the place where dogs licked the blood of Navot shall dogs lick your blood, as well."

And of his wife, God says...

"The dogs shall eat Ezevel in the moat of Yizrael."

This promise of God echoes in Achav's head...

When Achav heard those words, he rent his clothes and put sackcloth on his skin and fasted and lay in sackcloth, and went slowly.

After three years, Achav seems to think that God has forgotten and the threat of death fades. The story of Navot is almost forgotten. But, in the third year, an official royal visit takes places in Yizrael.

Yehoshafat the king of Yehuda came down to the king of Israel.

Yehoshafat is known as a righteous king. Probably the reason for his visit is to try to build good relations between the two Israelite kingdoms and their leaders in order to bring the ten tribes closer to Judaism.

Royal visits are known as occasions for good food and fine wine. At a certain point, wine takes over...

And the king of Israel said to his servants: "Do you know that Ramot Gilad is ours, and we are quiet about it? Why don't we take it out of the hand of the king of Aram?"

Under the high atmosphere the wine creates, the king turns to Yehoshafat.

"Will you go with me to battle to Ramot Gilad?"

King Yehoshafat mistakenly thinks that Achav speaks in general and so his answer, in general, is yes.

Yehoshafat said to the king of Israel: "I am as you are, my people as your people, my horses as your horses."

When Achav gives an order to the army to get ready to move, Yehoshafat understands that Achav means right now. And Yehoshafat tries to stall for time...

Yehoshafat said to the king of Israel: "Inquire please at the word of the Lord today."

Achav has no problem to ask the Lord's opinion, so he brings 400 prophets, and he asks them...

"Shall I go against Ramot Gilad to battle or shall I refrain?"

In one voice, the 400 men answer**...**

"Go up. The Lord will deliver it into the hand of the king."

Yehoshafat sees that these prophets are not exactly God's prophets. He can tell that these are pagan prophets Ezevel once had around her. So Yehoshafat tries again...

"Is there no longer here a prophet of the Lord, that we might inquire of him?"

And the king says...

"There is yet one man by whom we may inquire of the Lord, Micayahu, the son of Yimla. But I hate him. He does not prophesy good concerning me, but evil."

So Micayahu is asked to come to King Achav to address the question whether to go to war to take Ramot Gilad or not.

When he came to the king, the king said to him: "Micayahu, shall we go to Ramot Gilad to battle or shall we refrain?"

Very cynically, Michayahu talks to the king...

"Go up and prosper. The Lord will deliver it into the hand of the king."

The king gets angry...

"How many times shall I order you that you say to me only the truth in the name of the Lord?"

The Prophet Michayahu becomes very serious. And he says...

"Listen to the word of the Lord. I saw the Lord sitting on His throne and all the host of heaven standing by Him on His right side and on His left side.

The Talmud says that the spirit was no other than the soul of Navot, who has come to take revenge from Achav. (*Shabbat, p149*)

And the Lord said: "Who shall entice Achav, that he may go up and fall at Ramot Gilad."

And one said: "On this manner." And another said: "On that manner." And then the spirit came forward and stood before the Lord and said: "I will entice him."

And the Lord said to him: "How?" And he said: "I will go forth and will be a lying spirit in the mouth of all his prophets." And He said: "You shall entice him and shall prevail also. Go forth and do so."

The realistic picture the prophet gives the king does not impress the king, who is in a high mood and still anxious to go to the battle that he is not going to return from.

Instead...

The king said: "Put this fellow in the prison and feed him with poor bread and with bad water, until I come back in peace."

Very arrogantly, Achav takes his army and the army of Yehoshafat and marches his way to Ramot Gilad, which is to-day the Golan Heights, under the claim of taking back Israeli land from the hands of Aram. The rest of this story is described in the book of Kings 1, chapter 22 and is told in the story of the Golan Heights.

The prophecy of Eliyahu, regarding the vineyard of Navot, which has been taken by killing him, is about to hap-pen, just the way he said. Time has passed and Eliyahu passes his spirit to Elisha, his student. Elisha is the one who takes it on himself to bring the prophecy to fulfillment.

The Midrash reveals the name of the son of the Prophet who has been sent on this mission as Yona. (*Bamidbar Zuta, s1, c14*)

Elisha the Prophet called one of the sons of the proph-ets and said to him: "Gird up you loins. Take this jar of oil in your hand and go to Ramot Gilad."

When you arrive there, find Yehu, the son of Yehoshafat, the son of Nimshi, and go in and make him get up from among his colleagues. Bring him to an inner chamber.

From this description, we understand that the action should be confidential, secretive.

Then take the jar of oil and pour it on his head and say: "Thus says the Lord: I have anointed you king over Israel. Then open the door and flee. Do not linger."

Obviously, we can understand that this mission involves great risk.

So the young man, even the young man the prophet, went to Ramot Gilad. And when he came, behold, the captains of the host were sitting and he said: "I have a message for you, captain."

And Yehu said: "To which of us all?" And he said: "To you, captain."

And he arose and went into the house. He poured the oil on his head and said to him: "Thus says the Lord, the God of Israel: I have anointed you king over the people of the Lord, even over Israel. And you shall strike the house of Achav, your master, that I may avenge the blood of My servants the prophets, and the blood of all the servants of the Lord, at the hand of Ezevel.

"The whole house of Achav shall perish. I will cut off from Achav every male child, and anyone that survives him or that is left remaining in Israel. I will make the house of Achav like the house of Yerovam the son of Nevat, and like the house of Baasha the son of Achiyah. The dogs shall eat Ezevel in the portion of Yizrael. There shall be no one to bury her." And he opened the door and fled.

When Yehu leaves the house, a strange dialog of questions and answers takes place.

"Is all well? Why did this mad fellow come to you?"

Yehu responds in a strange manner.

"You know the man and what his talk was."

But the friends understand that something very important happened in the room and they ask...

"It is false. Tell us now."

Yehu lets them in on the secret.

"Thus says the Lord: 'I have anointed you king of Israel.'"

The impact of the new message is so powerful that even though these people were supposed to be loyal to Queen Ezevel as her servants...

Every man took his garment and put it under him on the

top of the stairs and blew the shofar, saying: "Yehu is king."

Yehu suggests kindly...

"If this is your will, then let no one escape and go out of the city, to go to tell it in Yizrael."

Yehu starts a revolt against the Queen Ezevel

And it looks like Yehu's personality is so charismatic that he doesn't have to order, just to suggest, for people to obey him instantly.

Now Yehu takes the people gathering around him towards Yizrael to take over the city and kill Ezevel and wipe out all of the house of Achav, just as Yona the Prophet ordered him to do.

So Yehu rode in a chariot and went to Yizrael.

When Yehu gets close to the city, the guards at the tower report of a company of strangers riding towards the city. At the same time, there is a royal visit in the city. The king of Yehuda, Achaziah comes to see Yoram, the son of Achav, who was injured in a battle with Aram on Ramot Gilad.

And so Yoram, also known as Yehoram, orders...

"Send a rider to meet them. Let him ask: 'Did you come in peace?'"

The rider meets Yehu and asks...

"Thus says the king: 'Do you come in peace?'"

Once again the response of Yehu is quite strange.

"What have you to do with peace? Come join my rear."

Not even a word about war or anything like this, but the message is clear.

From the tower in Yizrael, the guard reports...

"The messenger met them, but he did not come back."

So now a second rider is sent to meet Yehu and asks...

"Thus says the king: 'Do you come in peace?'"

Yehu responds the same way.

"What have you to do with peace? Come join my rear."

The guard on the tower reports that the rider met them,

but did not return.

Now the guard can identify the leader of the company by the way he rides...

"The driving is like the driving of Yehu the son of Nimshi. He drives recklessly."

From this description, we can understand that Yehu rides in a very special way, which was known to the people, especially in the city Yizrael. It seems like he spent time there. We are about to learn that he was one of the servants of Ezevel, maybe the very one that had to falsely testify against Navot.

At this point, King Yoram and King Achaziah go out and meet the company.

Yoram said: "Make ready." And they made ready his chariot. And Yoram, king of Israel and Achaziah, king of Yehuda went out, each in his chariot. They went out to meet Yehu and found him in the land of Navot the Yizraeli.

Yoram asks...

"Do you come in peace, Yehu?"

This time, Yehu responds roughly...

"What peace, as long as the harlotry of your mother Ezevel and her witchcrafts are so many?"

Yoram tries to back up...

Yoram turned his hands and flees, saying to Achaziah: "It is a trap, Achaziah."

But Yehu is quicker.

Yehu drew his bow with his full strength and struck Yoram between his arms. The arrow went out at his heart and he sunk down in his chariot.

King Achaziah tries to escape through the garden.

Yehu followed after him, and said: "Strike him also in the chariot."

Now Yehu enters into Yizrael to finish the job...

And when Yehu entered into Yizrael...

The First Lady of Yizrael is fully aware of what is happening. She analyzes her situation and understands that she is left with one card only, and that is her personal charm.

Ezevel heard it. She painted her eyes, adorned her head, and looked out the window.

When Yehu enters the city gate, she turns to him...

"Is it well, you Zimri, his master's killer?"

Yehu looks at her and asks her servants next to her one question.

"Who is with me? Who?"

The servants understand that they are running out of choices.

And Yehu adds...

"Drop her down."

The most attractive, manipulative pagan woman in Israel is pushed out of the window.

So they threw her down and some of her blood was sprinkled on the wall and on the horses.

Yehu steps on her with his horses as he enters into the palace.

She was trampled on under the horse's foot. When he came in, he did eat and drink.

During the meal, Yehu turns to his men saying...

"Look now after this cursed woman and bury her. She is a king's daughter."

It seems that after Ezevel was pushed out of the window and stepped on by the horses, the dogs jumped on her...

And they went to bury her. They found no more of her than the skull, the feet, and the palms of her hands.

Yehu's servants describe what they see and Yehu says...

"This is the word of the Lord, which He spoke by His servant Eliyahu the Tishbi, saying: 'In the land of Yizrael, the dogs will eat the flesh of Ezevel. The carcass of Ezevel shall be as dung upon the face of the field in the land of Yizrael, so that they shall not say: This is Ezevel.'"

Standing today on top of the hill of Tel Yizrael, over-looking the valley underneath, knowing that this is the place that hosted these unique personalities – Navot, Achav, Ezevel, Eliyahu, Yehu and the rest – is absolutely emotional!

There was something good about the wicked woman Ezevel, according to the Midrash.

The Midrash says that every time there was a wedding or a funeral in Yizrael, Ezevel would come out of her house, which was located in the center of the city and join the people, either celebrating or mourning. Because of this, her skull, her feet, and palms of her hands were spared from the dogs. *(Yalcut Shimoni, Kings 2, c232)*

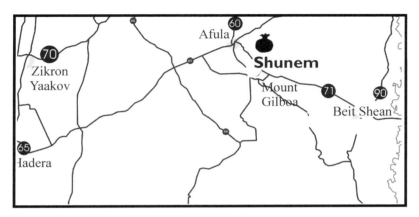

In The Time Of The Kings
Kings 2: 4

Shunem

The city Afula is known as the "Queen of the Valley" of Yizrael. Located in the middle of the valley, on a junction of major roads coming from the mountains of Shomron in the south, from the city Beit Shean in the east, the road to Haifa goes west and the road to the north goes to upper Galilee and the city Tzfat.

East of Afula there is a small Arab village called Sulem. This village sits on the ruins of the ancient Jewish city, Shunem. Easy to hear the connection between the names, the Arabs would preserve the Hebrew names, but pronounce them their way.

The city Shunem, during the time of the Kings in the First Temple period, is a place the Prophet Elisha comes to visit from time to time. One of the ladies of the city notices his arrival and offers him something to eat.

On a day that Elisha came to Shunem, there was a great woman. She asked him to eat bread. And so it was, whenever he passed by, he turned in there to eat bread.

The woman feels like she wants to give more...

She said to her husband: "Behold now, I know that this is a holy man of God, that passes by us often. Let us make, please, a little attic on the roof. Let us set up a bed there for him, a table, a stool, and a candlestick. It shall be that when he comes to us, that he shall turn in there."

The next time Elisha arrives in Shunem...

He turned into the upper attic and lay there.

Elisha thinks that maybe this woman needs something and this is the reason why she went to so much trouble for him.

"You have been so concerned for us with all this care. What can we do for you? Do you need to speak to the king or to the captain of the army?"

The woman answers simply...

"I dwell among mine own people."

This means she does not ask for anything. She is satisfied.

Then Gehazi, the Prophet's servant, remarks...

According to the Zohar, the first time Elisha used the attic the woman from Shunem built for him was Rosh Hashana. *(c231)*

"She does not have a son, and her husband is old."

Elisha calls her and as she stands at the door, he promises...

"At this time next year, you will embrace a son."

The woman responds...

"No, my lord, man of God, do not deceive your maidservant."

The time passes and the words of the Prophet come true.

The woman conceived and bore a son at the time Elisha had said to her.

As we can believe, this unexpected son was a source of joy and happiness for the woman and her husband. When he grows up...

He went out to his father to the grain cutters. When the day becomes hot, he said to his father: "My head, my head." And he said to his servant: "Carry him to his mother."

His mother...

...sat him on her knees until noon, and then he died.

The poor mother...

...went up and laid him on the bed of the man of God. She shut the door behind him and went out.

She understands that the time now is critical.

She called to her husband and said: "Send me, please, one of the servants and one of the asses so that I may run to the man of God and come back."

Her husband, who has no clue, asks...

"Why do you need to go to him today? It is neither new moon nor Shabbat."

Under different circumstances, she would explain, but now she only says...

"Shalom."

The instructions she gives the boy with her are strict.

"Drive and go forward. Do not stop for me unless I tell you."

Somehow, she figures out where to find Elisha.

So she went and came to the man of God in Mount Carmel.

Elisha notices her arrival...

He said to Gehazi his servant: "This is the Shunammite."

Elisha gives the order to Gehazi...

"Please run to meet her and say to her: 'Is all well with you? Is all well with your husband? Is all well with the child?'"

According to the Talmud, one of the major differences between Shmuel the Prophet and other prophets, excluding Moshe, was that Shmuel never asked anything of anybody and would not accept any favors, presents, or goods at all. *(Brachot, p10)*

The Shunammite ignores Gehazi...

When she came to the man of God on the hill, she caught

hold of his feet. Gehazi came to push her away, but the man of God said: "Leave her alone. Her soul is bitter within her. The Lord has concealed it from me, and has not told me."

The Shunammite's question shakes the earth and heaven...

"Did I ask you for a son? Did not I say:'Do not deceive me?'"

Elisha turns to Gehazi...

"Gird up your loins and take my staff in your hand and go your way. If you meet any man, do not salute him. If any salute you, do not answer him. Lay my staff on the face of the child."

According to the Zohar, the name of the Shunammite's son is Havakook.

The *gematria* of the Hebrew letters of Havakook includes one of the names of God.

So with the name of God, Elisha is able to bring his life back. *(c44)*

The Shunammite would not give up...

"As the Lord lives, and as your soul lives, I will not leave you." And he arose and followed her.

Elisha joins her...

Elisha comes into the house. The child is dead and laid upon his bed.

It looks hopeless, but...

He went in and shut the door and prayed to the Lord.

He went up and lay on the child and put his mouth on his mouth and his eyes on his eyes and his hands on his hands. He stretched himself upon him. The flesh of the child became warm.

Then he returned and walked in the house once, to and fro. He went up and stretched himself upon him.

And the child sneezed seven times and the child opened his eyes.

The boy is alive. His mother comes.

She went in and fell at his feet and bowed down to the ground. She took her son and went out.